Depression Visible:
The Ragged Edge

Diana Alishouse

Depression Visible: The Ragged Edge — © Diana Alishouse 2010

ISBN: 978-0-9818251-5-1

This book was printed in the United States of America

Journey of a Dream Press
PO Box 1565
Duluth, GA 30096
www.JourneyofaDream.com

Note from Author:

I have written about my experience and the things I have learned about depressive brain disorders. I do not claim to be a health care professional nor to be able to treat or counsel anyone who may have this or any other disorder or illness. This book is not intended as a substitute for professional medical care. Please consult a qualified physician about your own needs. I wish you well in your path toward wellness.

Acknowledgements

I have received help from many people through the years. They all had a hand in getting me to the point of publishing this book. Some with kicks in the behind, some with gentle nudges.

My friends in Beta Sigma Phi were the first to see my quilt, *The Ragged Edge*. They looked and listened as I described the meaning of the various parts and then surrounded me with hugs, tears, and encouragement to continue with my own form of expression.

Isabel Davidoff, Director of the D/ART Campaign, at the National Institute of Mental Health and her helper Valna Montgomery, Public Affairs Specialist, helped me learn that my *Ragged Edge* art quilts were worthy of being shown to a wide audience. They accepted them into the art show *Depression: From Darkness to Light* at the National Museum of Health and Medicine in Washington, D.C.

James Hawkins gave me his tie which I used to make the flag on the Ship of Fools quilt.

Jan Vaughn McCracken, Librarian, ordered many books and periodicals for me through the Colorado Interlibrary Loan Program.

Deb Ashley gave me the poems, *set adrift* and *untitled*, to include in the book.

Kathleen Sandberg gave me the phrase "pills and skills" to refer to the need for both medication and learning.

My parents, Walter E. and Tommie J. Stewart, gave me the very best upbringing they knew how to provide. I appreciate them for all they did to make me the person I am.

Dr. John Edwards of Vermont read an early draft of my book and gave me several pages of notes about anger. I have incorporated much of what he taught me into the book.

Dr. Malcolm Dickerson, who was practicing medicine in a small town in rural Colorado, accurately diagnosed my illness in 1985.

My loving mother-in-law Lennie Alishouse and her friends taught me how to make quilts.

Jennifer J. Goble, Ph.D., friend and counselor, assured me that I am an okay person—and a wonderful person. So is she.

D Bates and my NAMI Connections Support Group gave me the kick I needed to get this book published.

My daughter, Erica, bore the brunt of my anger, fear, hopelessness, and helplessness and became a wonderful woman anyway. I am so sorry for my inability to nurture her the way I wanted to, and I am so happy that she forgave me. I am still learning how to forgive myself.

My sister Fran Stewart, writer of the Biscuit McKee mystery series, gave me the poem *Patchwork* and relentlessly kept after me to publish this book. She even gave me to her publisher Darlene Carter at Doggie in the Window Publications.

My husband Marvin taught me by example how to think clearly before reacting emotionally. Without him I would not be alive. Thank you, Honey.

TABLE OF CONTENTS

Preface

This book is not a cry for sympathy for the victims of depression or bipolar illness. Anyone can be a victim of something, but claiming victimhood is being passive and helpless. We are not helpless, and we do not need to be passive.

Research abounds. There is more information available each year, and we are learning how to use that information to help those with depressive brain disorders. The more we learn, the more we realize that this so-called mental illness is really a physical illness. It is not some awful devil to whom we must play host. It is simply a common illness. If it is recognized, it can be treated—usually with excellent results.

But the sad truth is that many people who experience a depressive illness, whether in themselves or in their families, do not recognize the illness for what it is. Unless it is recognized, it cannot be treated.

Albert Camus said, "If the world were clear, art would not exist. Art helps us pierce the opacity of the world."[1] I want to "pierce the opacity," help you to imagine it so vividly that you will be able to recognize it when you see it. If you can do that, then you will be better able to help someone you know who has this illness—maybe even yourself.

The saying, "a picture is worth a thousand words" has a basis in fact. Eighty percent of the input routes of the nervous system are devoted to getting visual information to the brain. Fifty percent of our brain function is devoted to processing visual information. Our visual sense conveys more information of greater complexity than any other sense.[2]

I see means *I understand.*

Art is communication—direct, intuitive, and right-brained. Like music, it bypasses words. For me, the words tumble around too much and I get all confused. However, if I take a bit of cloth that means something because of its color, texture, or shape, and sew it down in a place that speaks to other bits of cloth, then I can fasten down those words and my thoughts. My quilts are my art and my way of sharing what I have learned about depression.

Why quilts? They take a long time to make. I could have just painted pictures. But I am dealing with emotions—feelings. A lot of the appeal of quilts is tactile—feeling. Nobody feels a painting. Nobody can resist feeling a quilt.

I feel means *I understand*.

Think about the traditional quilt patterns which were developed and used by our mothers and grandmothers. They were utilitarian, but also a necessary outlet in a time when female expression was limited. They have names like Flying Geese, Log Cabin, Courthouse Steps, Flower Basket, Drunkard's Path, and Wedding Ring. They are abstract designs. They are about significant things in our ancestors' lives. Their quilts speak to us and we feel their warmth, both literal and symbolic. We understand them instinctively, and we know of the love that went into their making.

My quilts are abstract designs of my own creation. They spoke to me as I was making them. They helped me understand. I count on them to speak for me, to convey what I cannot say in words. Picasso described art as "... a form of magic designed as a mediator between this strange hostile world and us, a way of seizing the power by giving form to our terrors as well as our desires."[3] My quilts accomplish this for me and, hopefully, you.

When the *Ragged Edge* series of quilts was shown at the National Museum of Health and Medicine in Washington, D.C. in 1991, one of the most frequently heard comments was, "I know what she was feeling when she made this quilt, because I've felt the same way." On another occasion, a young woman carefully studied the quilts then said, "These look just like my life."

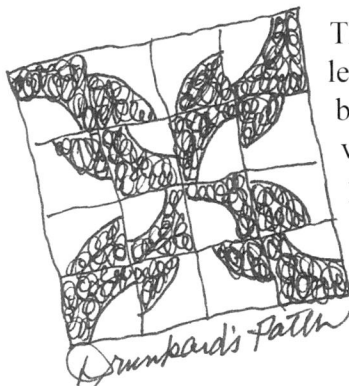
Drunkard's Path

There are hundreds of books about depressive illness. I've read and learned from many of them. To the best of my knowledge, this is the first book that shows what depressive illness feels like. This book makes the visual connection with all the descriptions and prescriptions. I invite you to see, to experience depression and wellness through the medium of my *Ragged Edge* series of art quilts.

Diana Alishouse
Colorado
2010

Basket Weave

Wind Mill

Attic Windows

Monkey Wrench

Chapter 1:
An Overview

Our emotions, our moods are part of what makes us human. We may feel happy, sad, elated, discouraged, angry, enraged, contented, afraid, joyful, disgusted, amused, anxious, embarrassed, helpless, loving. How many words are there in the English language that denote an emotion or a certain degree of an emotion? The spectrum of moods is wide, and all humans experience the roller coaster.

We all experience times when we are down in the dumps, and often we experience more serious periods when we are depressed because of circumstances. These reasons generally involve a loss of some sort, even though the loss may be significant only to the one who has experienced it. There is, at the very least, a short period of grief. A depression such as this, though painful, is usually a healthy way of dealing with loss. It is a time when we rely on our own inner strength of mind and spirit, and on our family and friends for help and understanding. After the grief period our mood lightens and we return to the middle part of the scale of human moods.

When we go through periods of elevated mood, we are very happy; we feel that life is wonderful, that things will go on blissfully forever. We are on a roll. But soon reality intrudes; we descend from our Olympian emotional heights and resume the middle range of our mood spectrum.

Sometimes, however, our emotional swings become greatly exaggerated and beyond our control. We may experience unpredictable and uncontrollable emotional swings, or we become stuck somewhere on the emotional chart. We then have what is called a mood disorder which is also known as an affective disorder. When this happens, we need more help than our family and friends are able to give.

The word "affect" is used to refer to a person's emotional tone. Affective disorders, then, are those which disturb the "affect" or mood, and they are generally divided into two categories: bipolar (manic-depressive) disorders and unipolar (depressive) disorders.

Simply put, **bipolar** disorders are characterized by excessive elation alternating with excessive unhappiness. This includes major depressive disorder and dysthymia (chronic depression). This form of illness used to be called manic-depression. **Unipolar** disorders, on the other hand, involve relatively long periods of excessive gloom or unhappiness.

This book is not about the ordinary and temporary blue moods which assail each of us from time to time. The term "depressed" is commonly used to refer to these brief periods:
"Oh, I've had the most depressing day."
"I'm so depressed. I didn't make the team (or get the job, or whatever)."
"I've been depressed ever since we moved here last month."
These down in the dumps moods are certainly real, but, generally, they resolve themselves.

The depression I refer to is not even one of those spiritually painful but necessary periods during which we reexamine our life, goals, beliefs, and habits. Those periods, though painful, may be ultimately beneficial by focusing us on what is not right in our lives so we can make changes. Usually, they are limited in duration and do not destroy our ability to act.

I am talking about a pervasive condition that goes way beyond merely being down in the dumps or having the blues. It is being stuck at a low point on the mood chart. It eats away at a person's mind and spirit until it causes severe problems—inability to care for one's self or spouse or children, divorce, job loss, underachievement in all aspects of life, verbal or physical abuse of others, alcoholism, substance abuse, episodes of outrageous violence, withdrawal from contact with others, and even suicide or murder.

ZIG ZAG

The blue and silver area is the normal range of mood variations.
Black and white outlined in red—abnormal, exaggerated, uncontrollable.
An illness.

Depression—alternating bands
of black and white
descending lower and lower into the dark confusion.
Red and black strings
pulling down down down maybe right out of life itself.
White handkerchief with flowers on it
my grief over the loss of Me.
The edge is ragged, unfinished, too tired to finish anything.
The red and black skull is suicide.

Manic—black and white dots like the effervescence of champagne rising rising rising
bubbling up and up where all is go go go and yellow sunshine and flowers
and the energy goes and flows and glows and flowers and glowers
get out of my way the edge is ragged, unfinished thoughts toofasttofinishanything.

The lavender cord pinned
on is the help I received
from OUTSIDE
which enabled me to get
from
depression
to
safety

sanity.

This illness has a terrible impact on our society. About 20.9 million American adults, or about 9.5% of the adult population in a given year have a mood disorder. Major depression is the leading cause of disability in the U.S. for ages fifteen to forty-four. It affects about 14.8 million American adults each year.[4]

According to a survey taken in July and August of 2002, and reported by the Depression and Bipolar Support Alliance in their quarterly newsletter *Outreach* in the Winter 2002-3 issue "…the majority of people are aware that mood disorders exist and cause problems, but far fewer actually know the facts about the illnesses and treatments." In addition:

• 29% believe that people with mood disorders do not live "normal" lives when treated
• 66% believe mood disorder medications are habit forming
• 19% believe people with mood disorders should not have children
• 22% believe people who take medication for mood disorders are weak or lazy
• 25% believe people with mood disorders are dangerous

It seems that in spite of tremendous educational efforts by the mental health community since that survey was done, the symptoms are often still seen only as evidence of some character defect, or as mere personal weakness or lack of will power. Sadly, we often believe these things about ourselves.

"Willpower? Shit! Don't talk to me about willpower. I use more willpower every second of every day just to keep from drowning myself than most people use in a lifetime."   D.A. journal entry

In my own case, I lived in a prison of more or less chronic depression for almost thirty years. There were only a few brief periods of normalcy or elation. My life was a series of disjointed starts and stops. For someone who started out as such a good, clever child, I became a huge disappointment to my family. All relationships were difficult. I made poor life decisions. I lived in a constant fog where I could never find my way, my direction. There was no sense to anything—only a yo yo life of revolving pain, numbness, fear, rage and helplessness. I was divorced twice. It was difficult for me to be a good parent—often impossible. I was never able to attain the success I knew I should have been capable of achieving in a career. As I look back I am appalled by so many of my thoughts and actions. How could I possibly have thought and acted that way? All that lost time and love and achievement!

My illness should have been recognized by doctors several times before it actually was. And my experience is common.

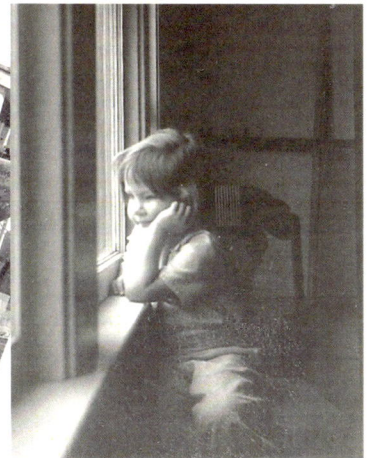

Chapter 2:
About Stigma

I n ancient Phoenicia, the "crazy people" were periodically loaded onto a rudderless ship and set adrift in the Mediterranean—a "ship of fools."[5]

In the Middle Ages the "ship of fools" was a symbol that meant a journey with no end, no safe destination, an endless going back and forth, an appropriate symbol for the condition of many people with mood disorder, both throughout history and now.

set adrift
by deb ashley

set adrift i have been
left for dead
like the other bits of trash in people's lives
deemed worthless by some
dangerous by others

not worth saving i am

all my talents lost to the world
doomed to be forever lost
alone
an outcast they cry
cast out cry i

alas they set me loose upon the sea
in this old and rotten ship

cast out of this world and into
the ship of fools

If I had lived earlier, I would still have been on that ship."   D.A. journal entry.

Occasionally, mental illness has been viewed as a physical illness. Medical books from ancient Egypt show that depression was recognized there 3000 years ago and was considered to have a physical cause.[6] In classical Greece, Hippocrates, the "Father of Medicine," believed that mental illness was caused by an imbalance of the four fluids or humors which made up the body. This idea gave rise to the practice of leeching or bleeding patients in order to restore balance, an ineffective and actually harmful cure.

This view of mental illness as having a physical cause was not the prevalent viewpoint throughout history. For the most part, it was an idea held by only a few of the most educated people of the time.

More often, people with mood disturbances, as well as other mental and physical illnesses, were seen as possessed by devils, or as witches, or as people being punished by the gods (or by God) for their transgressions, or as simply being bad people.

The Biblical story of King Saul in I Samuel is an example of terrible depression seen as divine punishment. At first, when Saul became mildly depressed, David was able to lift his spirits by playing music. "And it came to pass, when the evil spirit was upon Saul, that David took an harp, and played with his hand: so Saul was refreshed, and was well, the evil spirit departed from him."[7]

Early Greek legends show the gods, Zeus, Athena, Apollo, and the rest of that crowd, constantly mucking about in the affairs of man. They could cause fortune and misfortune, health and illness, sanity and insanity as a matter of favor or punishment or merely as a whim.[8]

The Dark Ages (476-1453), was a period of superstition and fear. The Devil was believed to be everywhere and was the source of most illness or abnormality. The mentally ill, especially, were perceived as being possessed by the Devil. They were believed to be the cause of numerous problems from sabotaging the food supply by causing milk to turn sour and hens to quit laying, to causing miscarriages and accidents. Predictably, methods of dealing with them were cruel. The Ship of Fools during this time was not just set adrift; the individuals on board were punished horribly, and often put to death.

In the 15th century, with the advent of the Renaissance, attitudes toward mental illness began to change. Institutions were built to house the "lunatic" and the poor—usually together.

By the 17th century, when the Scientific Revolution began, the belief in witches and possession had diminished, but it certainly had not disappeared. Indeed, the infamous Salem witchcraft trials occurred in 1692 at the very end of the 17th century.

During the 18th Century—the Age of Enlightenment—mental illness was still seen as shameful, something to be feared, ignored, and hidden away, if not actually persecuted. The insane were simply locked up with the criminals and chained to the walls of their prisons if they caused any trouble. In London's Bethlehem Royal Hospital, known popularly as Bedlam, sightseers were allowed to view the insane in the same way that we now go to the zoo to view the animals.

The 19th Century saw the beginnings of modern psychiatry as well as great advances in physical medicine. Emil Kraepelin carefully described symptoms of mental illnesses through exhaustive case histories, and classified mental illness as dementia praecox (schizophrenia), manic depressive psychosis, or paranoia.

The 20th Century, beginning with the publication of The Interpretation of Dreams by Sigmund Freud in 1900, has seen vast progress in knowledge about the varieties, symptoms, causes, and treatment of mental illness. Freud, whom we in America think of as linked with psychoanalysis, actually believed that the processes of mental illness would eventually be explained biochemically.

Passenger List [9]
Ship of Fools

Buzz Aldrin
Honore de Balzac
Hector Berlioz
John Berryman
Anton Bruckner
William Blake
Napoleon Bonaparte
Lord Byron
Albert Camus
Dick Cavett
Thomas Chatterton
Winston Churchill
Kurt Cobain
Samuel Coleridge
William Cowper
Hart Crane
Oliver Cromwell
Patty Duke
Thomas Eagleton
Edward Elgar
Carrie Fisher
F. Scott Fitzgerald
James Forrestal
Johann Wolfgang von Goethe
George F. Handel
Ernest Hemingway
Gerard M. Hopkins
William Inge
William James
Henry James

Randall Jarrell
Charles Lamb
Vivien Leigh
Primo Levi
Abraham Lincoln
Vachel Lindsay
Joshua Logan
Jack London
Robert Lowell
Salvador Luria
Martin Luther
Gustav Mahler
Herman Melville
Florence Nightingale
Sir Isaac Newton
Eugene O'Neill
Sylvia Plath
Edgar Allen Poe
Sergei Rachmaninoff
Theodore Roosevelt
Dante Rossetti
Giacchimo Rossini

John Ruskin
Robert Schumann
Alexandr Scriabin
Anne Sexton
Percy Bysshe Shelley
William Styron
Pyotr Ilyich Tchaikovsky
Alfred Tennyson
Ted Turner
Mike Tyson
Vincent van Gogh
Alice Walker
Mike Wallace
Virginia Woolf
Hugo Wolf

Psychologists and sociologists, as well as many laypersons, now think in terms of low self esteem, early childhood trauma, addiction, repressed anger, unresolved guilt, the stress of modern life, the breakdown of the family, and the exaltation of the individual. But, too often, problems are seen as essentially caused by the afflicted person's "badness." Many people see mental illness as a lack of good character, as God's will, or as a punishment for sins, and untreatable.

In 1999 a "… survey by the National Alliance for the Mentally Ill (now the National Alliance on Mental Illness) found that 71 percent of respondents thought severe mental illness was due to emotional weakness, 65 percent thought bad parenting was to blame, 35 percent cited sinful behavior, and 45 percent believed that the mentally ill bring on the illness and could will it away if they wished. Further, 43 percent believed mental illnesses are incurable, and only 10 percent thought that severe mental disorders had a biological basis and involved the brain."[10]

Better education is changing some of these perceptions, but, unfortunately, many people still hold on to such beliefs. Before scientific research found means of prevention and treatment, cholera, typhoid, bubonic plague, leprosy, and polio were subjected to the same types of misconceptions. This social stigma is, even today, one of the worst problems faced by the passengers on the Ship of Fools.

These, along with millions of not-so-famous people, including myself, have experienced depressive or bipolar illness. We must recognize our illness to get correct treatment for it. We must do this in spite of the stigma of badness and shame which is too often attached to mental illness. We must do what we can to eliminate that stigma, and end our endless journey on the Ship of Fools. We must find our direction, our harbor. Then we can disembark and live in harmony with ourselves and our fellow men and women.

One day in 1985 I went to a routine yearly appointment with my doctor. The day before, I had noticed a sidebar titled "Biologically Caused Depression" in a magazine. I clipped it and took it with me to the doctor. I waited in his examining room in my paper gown. When he came in I held out the clipping, began to cry, and said, "Do you think this is what is wrong with me?"

I was extremely lucky. He was a general practitioner who was up-to-date on depressive illnesses. "I don't know," he said. "But we will find out." He and his nurse took turns coming into the examining room where I sat and cried through three hours and a whole box of tissues. When I could finally talk coherently he explained about differential diagnosis—how he had to rule out many other physical conditions that have depression as a symptom before he could be sure that what I had was primary depression. He and his nurse stayed after hours and gave me a complete exam, took blood and urine samples, asked lots of questions about family history and my history. They made an appointment for me to come back the next day with my husband.

By that time he seemed fairly confident that I had a biologically based depression. He talked to my husband. "She's like your old truck, Marvin. When it breaks down you don't throw it away. You fix it." We decided to fix me. He prescribed an antidepressant, lithium (a mood stabilizer in case I was bipolar), and counseling. He called me regularly to monitor my progress

It was a good start, but it wasn't enough. I tried to be better. Oh, how I tried. I guess I was a little better, but it was mostly acting. I tend to do that. The doctor gave me some medicine and listened to me talk, so I got "better" just because I "knew" I was supposed to. He thought I was better than I actually was.

My journal entries show that I was still depressed. The same thoughts were churning round and round in my head, never being resolved:

"... and my hope of achieving anything other than just getting through one day at a time is dead. If I could have seen ahead, seen the futility of it all, I would have gone ahead and jumped off the roof that horrible night when I was in college."   DA journal 7/28/85

"I felt happy all day yesterday. I woke up happy this morning."   DA journal 7/30/85

"Here I am crying again. Woke up leaking at the eyeballs."   DA journal 8/1/85

It wasn't until several years later when I had another crying fit in another doctor's office that I was given a larger dose of my antidepressant medication. Then I really started to climb out of that hole of depression. The change was like a miracle. Within a few weeks I began wondering how I had fallen into that hole in the first place. Life was suddenly so full of color and movement. Jokes were silly. I could laugh. I could enjoy, actually enjoy, the most routine activities. My wardrobe and my house changed from pale beige and blue to vivid black and white, and red, and purple, and bright blue. And I wondered: how could I possibly have been so completely and thoroughly miserable for so long?

Drug therapy was and is still the key part of my treatment. But my treatment has also involved psychological counseling, and cultivating new habits, and learning a new way of thinking, since a lot of my previous assumptions about life were influenced or caused by my depression. I have worked hard on reinventing my physical, emotional, cognitive, social, and spiritual self.

That "black hole" is still down there and I could fall into it. But I have learned a great deal about how to avoid it. I am still learning how to take care of myself and how to know when to get help with taking care of myself.

When I reached a certain point in my process of learning how to be happy, I became angry that I had already spent half of my life in a depressed state. It was only by sheer luck that I had finally been diagnosed correctly. I decided then to use my experience to help other people with this disorder find out what is wrong with them so they can get treatment. I also want to join with others to erase some of the stigma attached to this type of mental illness.

There are many people working for this cause. In addition to those involved in the organizations listed in the Appendices, there are the researchers in universities, foundations, and pharmaceutical companies around the world, the health professionals who actually care for patients, the volunteers who organize and facilitate support groups, and the growing numbers of individuals who have told of their own experiences with mood disorders. We are many. We are making a difference.

Chapter 3:
Symptoms of Depression

Symptoms of Depression Can Include:

Persistent sad or "empty" mood

Loss of interest or pleasure in ordinary activities

Decreased energy, fatigue, being "slowed down"

Sleep disturbance (sleeping too much or too little)

Appetite and weight changes (either loss or gain)

Difficulty concentrating, remembering, making decisions

Feelings of guilt, worthlessness, helplessness, irritability

Thoughts of death or suicide, suicide attempts

Chronic aches and pains that don't respond to treatment

This is the usual list of symptoms of depression. It is certainly accurate. It is necessary, objective, and dispassionate. But it is only one sense of what depression is like. This clinical list could be etched on the heart of someone suffering from depression, yet that person could still be unable to connect the list with their own symptoms, with their own need for help.

There is another, deeper sense of depression — the subjective one. We must learn to look and listen for this more subjective view.

To be able to recognize the symptoms of depressive illness, we must be able to make a connection between that clinical list and the actual subjective experience of the illness. We must learn to "see the forest, not the trees;" we must recognize the pattern which makes up the illness. It really isn't that difficult to understand what those symptoms sound and look like in real life.

"THE RAGGED EDGE"

The metal part is the illness, the depression.
Inverted triangle... unstable.
Hard, cold. Screen distorting the view of the Black Hole, making it difficult to see.
The illness is difficult to diagnose.
Strings, thongs, wires...stuff.
This illness clutches, tangles, grabs, always there to snatch me back.

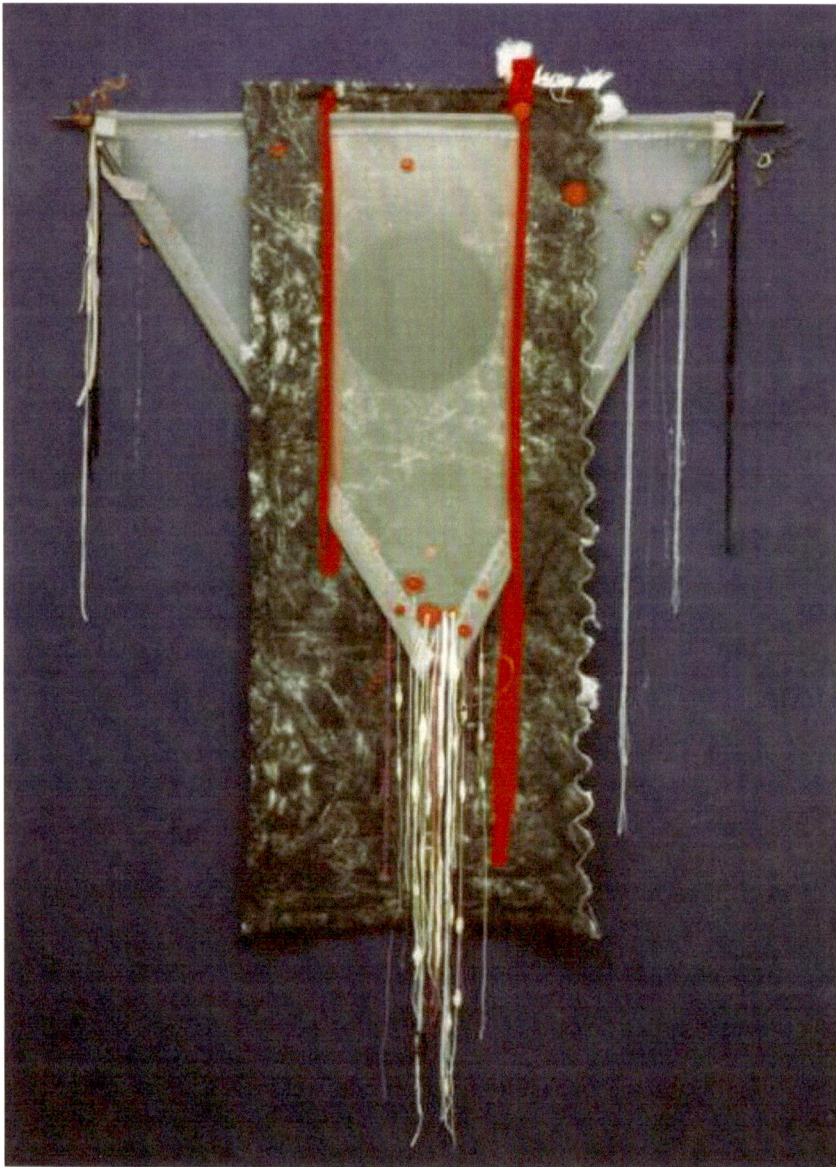

It is an illness, not a lack of character or will power.

The fabric part is the person.

Hanging there hurtful, red wounded, fastened by the red buttons, can't escape, like the buttons in my mind that keep getting pushed.

Mottled black cloth and gray whorl beads— thoughts round and round and bad and confused and what is it all for anyway?

Black, black circle at the center
the Black Hole
the void that is not IN me
the void that IS me

the place where I am, the what I am—helpless, hopeless,
I don't want to be.

Tiny blackened silver heart
lost.

Held by the illness.
Tiny blackened Hand of Fatima
my luck's
run out.
What luck?

Cocoons...
my talents and abilities....
wrapped,
hidden,
held away from me
by this illness,
this physical condition,
this altered brain chemistry.
Damn!
why?

I have heard so many people talking about their loved ones, friends, co-workers, saying things like: "What on earth is the matter with Jane/John? All she ever wants to do is sit at home and do nothing. She cries a lot. She's gained so much weight. (Or she's lost so much weight.) He's so angry. He's so crabby all the time. She's no fun to be with anymore. She's always so disgusted with everything. She always complains. He gets so upset over simple things. She sure never has anything good to say about anything or anybody. Oh, man, do we have to invite Her? She's such a drag. All she ever wants to talk about are her personal problems and her aches and pains. If she feels so bad, why doesn't she go to the doctor and do something about it. Well, she goes to the doctor a lot but they never seem to do her any good. He says he can't sleep well. (Or he just wants to sleep all the time.) She's so quiet and withdrawn. He's been drinking and fighting a lot.. Well, I just wish she would snap out of it and be happy. I'm getting sick and tired of putting up with that pissy attitude all the time."

When I hear people talking like this, I want to scream at them. "Wake up! See the pattern you have just described! You are listing symptoms of depressive illness. Your friend needs medical help. She/he can get well again and enjoy life. Please help her/him."

The idea that Jane/John could snap out of it and be happy if only she/he would exert some will power is an example of the attitude that mental illness is caused by some sort of innate badness or weakness within the person. This attitude, if expressed, only reinforces the depressed person's sense of inadequacy and failure, even though it may be offered in a spirit of helpfulness and love.

"Dear Diana, we have both analyzed our families and, as far as we know there is no manic depression. If you are willing to try it, we would like for you to come home for a few days just to renew some family ties. You do not have a monopoly on manic depression--there are so many confused people in the world today. But! You do have the stamina, the strong character and the determination to get this out of your system. So put your mind to it and do it. We love you very much and we hurt when you hurt. Love, Mama and Daddy." 3/87

The symptoms actually fall into three categories. There are thinking symptoms and acting symptoms and relationship symptoms. Sometimes the symptoms seem to fit in more than one category, but I still find these three useful when I work at figuring out what is going on in my head.

THINKING SYMPTOMS are also known as cognitive distortions.

- A persistent sad or "empty" mood, a gloomy or pessimistic outlook. Feeling guilty, thinking that you are worthless, helpless, and hopeless. A pervading sense of failure and inadequacy. Slowed thinking, difficulty in concentrating and remembering, indecisiveness. Rumination. Thoughts of death and/or suicide.

- *"I feel bored, bothered. What the hell is it all for, anyway."* D.A. journal entry

- Pooh Bear: "Why, what's the matter?"
  Eeyore: "Nothing, Pooh Bear, nothing. We can't all, and some of us don't. That's all there is to it."
  Pooh Bear: "Can't all what?"
  Eeyore: "Gaiety. Song and dance. Here we go round the mulberry bush."[11]

- What Jane's/John's friends say: "What on earth is the matter with Jane? She always seems so disgusted with everything. She always puts herself down. She takes everything so personally. He's no fun to be with anymore. She's so crabby all the time. She's so quiet, never talks anymore. It's hard to carry on a conversation with him."

- *"Nothing is fun. I don't enjoy anything. I might as well die."* D.A. journal entry

- I've suffered from depression a lot. The most horrible feeling is not wanting to live and not being able to act." Alice Walker, author of *The Color Purple*[12]

- *"Most often I didn't really want to commit suicide. That is active and was something I just couldn't manage. I just wanted to BE dead--a very passive state, peaceful, lacking pain."* D.A. journal entry

- Life is hard and then you die.

Depressed people can't see anything good or positive within themselves or in the things going on in their environment. They wallow in their own miserable viewpoint, seeing themselves as bad, ugly, inferior, incompetent, unlikeable, and undeserving regardless of any history of achievement or periods of normal mood ranges. They may imagine their world to be mean and out to get them.

Rumination is a habit of thinking that is very common in depressed people. The term itself is taken from the field of biology. Cows are ruminants. They have four stomachs. They regurgitate food, chew it again, swallow it again. It's how they digest their food. Depressed people tend to do the same thing with their thinking. It's as if the thoughts get "into the system," get trapped, and continue to go round and round—a perpetual feedback circle. People are not cows and shouldn't ruminate—either in their digestion or in their thoughts—but depressed people do it all the time. Some of us do it out loud, constantly and boringly rehashing the litany of all our problems. Some of us only do it silently.

"Stuff just goes round and round in my head. The same thoughts over and over and over." D.A. journal entry

My thought symptoms included cognitive distortions and rumination. I was hopeless, helpless, afraid and indecisive to the point that I could not even decide what clothes to wear. I carried the guilt of the world in my head. No matter what was wrong, it was somehow my fault that it didn't get fixed. There was nothing in life that I enjoyed. It consisted only of dragging myself out of bed each morning and dragging myself through a repetitive obstacle course each day so that I could drag myself back to bed at night.

Shattered Red is the only one of these quilts that I worked on while I was deeply depressed. It is not well crafted. Good quilting techniques didn't matter. I didn't realize it at the time, but making it was a desperate attempt to try to hold myself together. As I sewed the fractured pieces of reds together (the background), I had no plan for the final quilt. I remember thinking that I felt like that jumbled mess of red. Others have told me that during that time they had no hint that anything was wrong with me. They said I seemed "so normal... a little tired, maybe, but normal." How can that be? "A little tired"? I felt exhausted, drained. "Normal"? Inside I alternated between absolute hopelessness and absolute rage. I sewed those little pieces of cloth together not knowing what they were for, clutching at something, anything, just trying to hang on even though I couldn't think of a good reason why I should.

SHATTERED RED

How, at the same time, can I feel so much emptiness,
but also, so much rage and disgust and sadness?

Hot colors—reds, orange, pinks—rage and frustration.
Rage at myself and my confusion,
and at those close to me,
and at all the world in general,
and at God in particular.
Frustration—no direction, no coherent pattern to life.

Tiny green bits—tiny and very rare bits of peace that came to me somehow
Thank you, God.

The white grid overlaying the reds represents the regular pattern of daily life. This grid, super-imposed over my depression, was something for me to cling to and depend on. It felt boring, unrewarding, and totally devoid of even the simplest sense of pleasure. But it was busy, and it got me through the day.

White lightning flashes....terror...Oh, God, please,
I can't...
keep it together...
I'm going to shatter...
into
a million bits
of
nothing, fly   apart
into all
directions
at

once.

ACTING SYMPTOMS

- Loss of interest and pleasure in usual activities. Decreased energy, fatigue, being "slowed down." Being irritable, anxious. Suicide plans or attempts. Alcohol or substance abuse. Chronic aches and pains that don't respond to treatment. Sleep disturbance, appetite or weight change. Declining work performance.

- "I used to be self-motivating, a real go getter."—statement made by a depressed friend

- What Jane's/John's friends say: "She cries a lot. He never wants to do anything. He's always so disgusted with everything. All she ever wants to talk about is her personal problems and her digestion and her aches and pains. He just sits around and does nothing all the time. She's gained (or lost) so much weight. He can't sleep. She sleeps all the time. She's always complaining about something."

- Suicide—attempted or successful

These acting symptoms may seem obvious, but many people desperately try to cover up, to hide their depression. It doesn't take much acting ability to reply to the rhetorical, "Hi, how are you?" with a cheery sounding, "Fine, thanks. How are you today?" Sometimes the negative changes in actual behavior are the last symptoms to appear.

I have read separate estimates that half the patients who see family practitioners are suffering from some type of psychiatric problem and that sixty percent or more of the visits to general medical doctors are made by patients who have an emotional rather than an organic basis for their physical symptoms. Those aches and pains and digestive upsets are real.

My own symptoms included physical ones such as headaches, fatigue, digestive upsets, muscle spasms in my back and neck, irregular menses, sleep disturbance, and weight gain. Every time I would go down into another episode of depression, most or all of these symptoms would occur. I went to a lot of doctors. I was checked for ulcers, colon cancer, gout, and pregnancy. I was given muscle relaxers, Valium (this is a central nervous system depressant which hammered me down even further into my Black Hole), pain pills, stretching exercises, traction, a hysterectomy and ulcer medication. Each doctor I consulted asked only about the one specific complaint I was there for. Not one of them ever attempted to find out if there might be a larger pattern of symptoms. It is probable that many times I was evaluated simply as a hypochondriac.

I drank a lot. It was an attempt at self treatment. A drink or two (or three or...) lightened me up, made things more bearable, brought on a giggle now and then.

Altered sleep pattern is one of the common physical symptoms of depression.

THE ROOSTER CROWS TOO EARLY

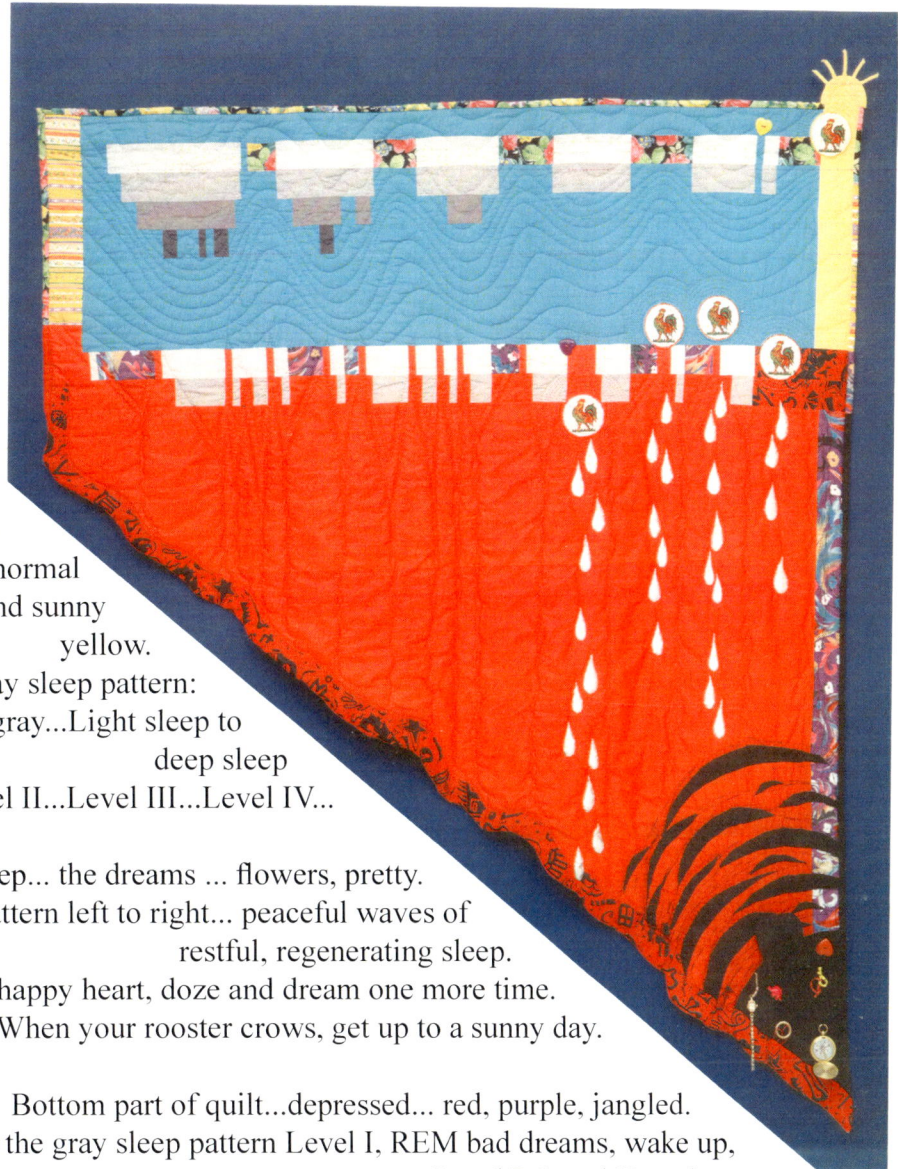

Top part of quilt... normal
...peaceful blue and sunny
yellow.
See the gray sleep pattern:
Light gray to dark gray...Light sleep to
deep sleep
Level I...Level II...Level III...Level IV...

See the REM sleep... the dreams ... flowers, pretty.
Follow the sleep pattern left to right... peaceful waves of
restful, regenerating sleep.
Wake up with a happy heart, doze and dream one more time.
When your rooster crows, get up to a sunny day.

Bottom part of quilt...depressed... red, purple, jangled.
See the gray sleep pattern Level I, REM bad dreams, wake up,
Level I, Level II, wake up...
all night long.
and the knotted threads and red and black,
and into the Black Hole where I really live...
please, God,
what is this all for?
why can't I just not be?

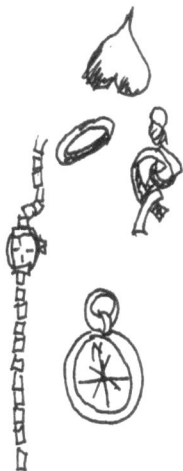

Trapped in the black hole are some of my lost valuables:
A red heart....energy, vitality, liveliness, health.
A golden ring... marriage, a sense of wholeness.
Twist ties...the ties that bind us to our friends and family.
A broken watch...lost time.
A compass.....lost sense of direction in life.
Fuschia colored dinosaur.... what could be more silly?
This is the loss that hurts the most: there is no humor left in life,
no silliness,
no giggles.

Suicide has been called a permanent solution to a temporary problem. Yes, that is true, but when you are feeling totally hopeless, it can seem to be the only way out of the dreadful pain.

In addition to the general symptoms of depression, there are some other signals of a possible impending suicide attempt. First and most important: it is NOT true that if a person talks about it, they won't do it. That is a really stupid idea that has somehow gotten into the current collective consciousness. If a person talks about suicide, they are thinking about it, may attempt it, and may succeed. Watch for statements such as, "Everybody would be better off without me" or "I just can't go on."

At the very least, a suicide attempt is a desperate cry for help.

Other signs of suicidal intentions are making final arrangements, putting business, financial, or personal affairs in order, giving away meaningful possessions, or making preparations as if getting ready to go away on a trip.

If you suspect the possibility of suicide, talk to the person. Ask if that is what he or she is planning. Find out how far the plans have been carried out. Let that person know that you care. Help him or her get medical help immediately. Suicide is preventable.

When I was a junior in college I overheard a comment from two of my roommates' rap session: "If you have nothing to live for, then you might as well not live." *Oh yes!!! Bullseye!!! I screamed and ran out of the house. Spent half the night walking around trying to figure out what to do. Went to the hospital "where they help people. I'll go in and ask at the front desk for someone to help me." So I went in, but since it was about 2 or 3 AM there was no one at the front desk. Panic. What to do? The janitor is staring at me. Get on elevator, push UP, doors close, UP, stop. People in white get on, stare at me. Stop, doors open, they get off. I go up up up to rooftop solarium crying, and no one to help, want to stop, not be. God, why does it hurt so bad and why am I so lost? why why why why why why why why why why wh can't get through the glass.*

People come and grab me and take me to the emergency room. They ask me dumb questions, "Have you been drinking? Did you have a fight with your boyfriend? What's your student ID number?"

They give me a shot and take away my clothes and tuck me in bed. Warm and cozy but I'm settled down just enough to stay awake and write poetry.

> *Go into thy closet and pray*
> *Everything will be okay.*
> *Don't worry.*
> *Just pray.*

And

> *Loneliness*
> *One hell of a Sunday*
> *Sky pissing little white chunks*
> *Fly TWA and go to Shitland*
> *My soul is as gray as the weather today*
> *Everything surrounds me*
> *But there is nothing*
> *I am here all of me alone*
> *Skin holds me in*
> *And I am separate from all without*
> *Everything swirls*
> *But nothing touches me*

The only thing that kept me alive later during my worst periods was the thought that committing suicide was something that I just could not do to my daughter. This, fortunately, had an ultimately happy result in our case. But I think I can guess very accurately at the emotional state and the thoughts of the perpetrators of family murder/suicide cases that are reported on the news. I can't stand to think about what might have happened in my own life. There was also one other factor—a tiny, tiny glow of, yes, curiosity. What will happen next in this soap opera life? How will all this crap end?

RELATIONSHIPS SYMPTOMS

Relationship symptoms are sometimes expressed as not wanting to be with other people. This may be especially noticeable if a previously friendly, gregarious person gradually becomes withdrawn. As my friend Jim put it, "I wanted to avoid being with others, particularly people I didn't know well, and yet I dreaded being alone with myself where I knew I would just wallow further into misery and despair."

It is also possible that having a lot of problems with family, friends, and/or co-workers could be an indicator of depression. It is, at least, an indication that depression should be considered as a cause. We generally do not recognize difficulties with personal interactions or problems at work as symptoms of depression. It is much easier to simply blame other people for causing problems or the pressure of work being more than we can handle.

Remember poor King Saul? As I read his story I know how overwhelmed he was with guilt and how hopeless and alone he felt. I also see that his relationships with others were affected. His servants, his friends, his son, even his God, seemed to have turned away from him. And, in fact, maybe they did, though not as soon as Saul imagined

Depressed people are hell to get along with. They are, in general, extremely pessimistic, critical of others and themselves, sad, withdrawn, and irritable. They are a real drag to be around. If you know someone like this, it is very likely that you are dealing with a person with a depressive illness, not someone who is simply being hard to get along with or who just has a rotten personality. This person needs medical help and needs your understanding and support.

People often think they are depressed because of the problems they have with relationships. That is not true. They have it backwards. People have those problems with relationships because they are depressed.

For example, I actually agreed to marry my second husband after he had given me two black eyes. If I had not been depressed I would not ever have married someone like that. That marriage was a problem which I bought into because of my depression.

A friend thinks he lost his business because he couldn't get a bank loan. I would say that he couldn't get the bank loan because he was exhibiting so many symptoms of depression that his previously cordial relationship with the loan officer was affected.

It is the symptoms themselves, whether they have to do with thinking or acting or relationships, that make it extremely difficult, if not impossible, for many depressed people to express accurately and coherently what is wrong with them. We must learn how to figure it out by paying careful attention to what they say and what they do.

If you dig through the layers of problems (stress, alcohol or substance abuse, trouble with relationships, lack of direction, feelings of despair, hopelessness, sleep difficulties, business or career failures, etc.), it may be that depression is at the core. If this is so, then when the depression is treated, the problems will either dissolve or be dealt with more effectively.

untitled
by
deb ashley

how can it be that i remain here
alone
locked behind this shattered wall of self
if i were stronger not so tired
i would try to open the door
but i am so tired and the
world keeps racing on
without me
all alone
tired
me

What do I want to do today? I can't figure out what I want to do.

Gray & gloomy out. Woke up sad. Feel bored. Need enthusiasm for something.

I'm so tired. Kinda down and plopped back into old habits.

Oh why bother?

I'm like a yo-yo and can't figure out what the string is that spins me up and down. Why am I here? What am I supposed to do?

Nothing to say. Or rather, Too much to say and don't know where to start.

see how to think I can figure

different Tonite. it act Tomorrow.

Chapter 4:
Symptoms of Mania

In the bipolar form of affective disorder, excessive elation alternates with depression. These "highs" can be even more disruptive than the depressive phase.

Symptoms of mania can include:

> Excessively "high" mood
> Irritability
> Decreased need for sleep
> Increased energy and activity
> Increased talking, moving, and sexual activity
> Racing thoughts
> Disturbed ability to make decisions
> Grandiose notions
> Tendency to be easily distracted

This is the clinical list of full blown manic symptoms. It helps, though, to think more in terms of a continuum of moods.

On the way up, out of the depths of despair and depression, or even just rising a little above the average range of human emotion, one can go through a hypomanic state. Hypomanic means just a little bit manic. A description of the actions and thought patterns of someone in this state is a description of many of our super achievers, our stars.

It is an emotional state of increased energy, drive, and competence, and fluency of thought and words. It is being on a roll. Many of Vincent Van Gogh's masterpieces were painted while he was in a hypomanic state. I wonder if this is how Rossini wrote *The Barber of Seville* in only thirteen days or how Handel composed *The Messiah* in only six weeks.

FLIPPED UP

Black and white squares the checkered flag at the finish line.
We are not only in the race, we are win place or show.
We are good at what we do, whatever we do.
We get things done.
We achieve.

We are primary colors—uncomplicated.
We are red—heroes and energy,
We are yellow—optimism and enthusiasm,
We are blue—well thought, well said.
Royal blue arrow—a sense of direction.
American flag—Teddy Roosevelt.

We are *CREATIVE* at what we do, whatever we do.
CREATIVITY BLOOMS.
See the tiny yellow letter "A" at the top. It stands for me,
Alishouse.
This is where I like to live.

See the triangle buttons.
Yellow and white buttons—Right side up the triangle is very stable.
Black button—Upside down it is very unstable.
This flipped up state can change unpredictably into flipped out mania
Or into depression.
Uh oh.
Maybe trouble.

What I think of as my creative tizzy is possibly a mild hypomanic phase. The ideas, associations, and linkages come easily and quickly, requiring me to go into a sort of over-drive to capture them all before they get away. In this rush I feel excited, I sweat, I forget to eat or sleep, I am unaware of time. I have plenty of energy. I feel extremely capable and pleased with myself. I go into high gear and I get a lot of work done. I think of it as being flipped up. Many people like their hypomanic swings.[13] I certainly do. But mine are limited in intensity and duration. I do come back down to earth—or, at least, I have so far.

In people with the full fledged bipolar disorder, hypomania is only a brief experience on the way to an extremely destructive mania. Reason and self control are lost. Binges of buying may bankrupt a family. Binges of travel or sex or anything else which may grab the person's attention are not limited by normal bounds of physical tiredness. I have read that be-fore treatment was available, fifteen percent of the people in a full blown manic state died of physical exhaustion.[14] There is also a distinct possibility of death by dumb stunts if a person in this state gets the notion that he is capable of flying or of stopping freight trains.

The manic person perceives himself to be in perfect control of himself and his en-vironment. Unfortunately, someone stuck in this emotional state is not in control and must often be forcibly restrained in order to prevent harm to himself or to others.

Learning plays a vital role in dealing with manic episodes. If we learn what triggers them and strive to be aware of when we begin to percolate a little too much, we can take steps to avoid the devastating results. In some cases we should sign a contract with a trusted friend or counselor giving them authority to intervene to prevent a dangerous episode.

"In October I become depressed. In March I become hypomanic. I think I am a bipo-lar II, linked to the sun." D.A. Journal

Oh my!
A mess!
A real nut!

flying in all directions at once
distracted distractive
jumbled racing thoughts and words go
can't stop
skull death danger
boats, ships, buildings, cars, roads, planes
binges of
drinking and
drugging and
spending and
traveling and
buying and
sex and.....

buttons and buttonholes don't match up.
this person makes no sense,
and everything is all at once.
yellow slash and safety pins cracked up
yellow the color of raving lunacy with
not much holding

it

together.

Chapter 5:
Causes of Mood Disorder

Is this depression a software problem (psychological) or a hardware problem (physical)? Which came first, the chicken or the egg? This is one of the issues that researchers have been dealing with. Some have argued for a purely physical cause; others have seen it as purely psychological in nature; some have reasoned that it has social or spiritual causes. These divisions certainly have merit as a basis for research, but while we wait for the scientists to discover a definitive cause, or causes, we know there is no way that a living person can be divided up into discrete physical, emotional, cognitive, social, and spiritual entities.

In my quilt, "Monkey Wrench," my separation of causes into the duality of psychological and physical is an oversimplification. I have included emotional, cognitive, social and spiritual factors as part of the psychological side since they become so embedded in our thoughts that we cannot distinguish whether we think something because of a supposedly innate psychological quality (personality or temperament or IQ, for example) or because we have nonconsciously soaked it up from our social interactions.

PSYCHOLOGICAL CAUSES OF DEPRESSION

We are assailed daily in the popular media with information about psychological causes of depression. Who has not heard of abuse, trauma, stress, rejection, failure, personality type, low self esteem, and learned helplessness? The principal focus in this country has been on trying to understand psychological problems.

By now, it seems obvious to us that a child who is listened to, understood, accepted, and affirmed will turn into a happier adult than a child who is unappreciated, manipulated, and taught lessons of powerlessness. This is a very simple view of the way early childhood experiences can affect our future mental health, yet it encompasses much of what has been found to be true about psychological causes for depression.

MONKEY WRENCH

White/brain/physical and black/mind/psychological
hooked together but not one,
not whole...
Somehow a monkey wrench has been thrown into my works.

See the black thoughts repeat,
Ruminate round and round, over and over, grinding me down.
My red psychological buttons keep getting pushed,
Initiating sequences of thoughts:
Same song, second verse.
Can't get better,
So it's gotta get worse.
Try to form a new pattern. Can't.
Can't think anything new.
Can't get loose.

The black thoughts are made of learned helplessness, low self esteem, pessimism, anger,
frustration, loss, trauma, hopelessness, emptiness, and philosophical uncertainty.

See the other side of the hook—white/brain/physical.
My genes, my biochemistry.
Chromosomes?Neurotransmitters? Neuroendocrines?
Too much alcohol?
Not enough exercise? Environmental poisons?
Vitamins?
Too much? too little?
Whaaaat?

Black/mind/psychological and White/brain/physical
which is cause?
and which is effect?

We learn much of our basic style of reacting to events and people in our world from our early caregivers.[15] If we see them showing fear and suspicion of other people and of events, then that is how we will learn to react. Our basic style of viewing the world will become one of pessimism. We will learn to assume the worst. We will see life as hopeless. Hopelessness is a major symptom of depression.

Learned helplessness is also important as a factor in later depression. A child who learns that she cannot have any effective control over what happens to her is a case of depression just waiting to happen. A feeling of helplessness is a major symptom of depression. If we learn to feel that way as children, then we have learned an enormous lesson in how to be depressed.

The ability to deal with anger, both our own and that of others, is a very necessary social skill which many depressed people have simply never learned. This is associated, oddly enough, with a lack of assertiveness. Angry people are aggressive, not assertive. The anger is bottled up—tightly corked—but when it gets too close to the surface it can explode with devastating consequences. All that trapped, unused anger eats away at every aspect of our lives.

Rumination is another habit of thinking that is learned early, along with a basic pessimistic attitude and a pervasive feeling of helplessness. If we are both hopeless (nothing will ever be good) and helpless (there is nothing I can do about it) then where can our thoughts go except around and around in circles—constantly rehashing the trash in our lives. Our thinking gets all screwed up by our emotions. We skip from one negative thought to another, unable to stop our own distorted views of ourselves and our world.

"I'm afraid of being insane, afraid of asking for help, afraid of thinking, 'What's the matter with me?' Am I crazy? Why do I think all this garbage? Why can't I stop?" D.A. Journal Entry

We look desperately to other people for support, comfort, approval and reassurance, but by this time there can never be enough to fill up our emptiness. And so, we are frustrated and angry as we feel them backing away from the emotional pit that is us. And we are back at the beginning: hopeless and helpless and alone. We are unable to act, only able to think, and unable to stop thinking. Round and round.

It doesn't matter whether these learned traits arise from isolated traumatic events or from repeated subtle conditioning. The brain/mind becomes organized in a depressive pattern. This pattern formation may be either tempered by or emphasized by our innate characteristics of personality, intelligence, and temperament.

SOCIAL CAUSES OF DEPRESSION

Depression has always been present. It can even be seen among populations of animals other than humans. Anything in a society that causes stress can cause depression—not in all the members, but certainly in the physically vulnerable ones. Some of these factors are low social status, poverty, violence, sudden changes, fear—the list is long.

Of course, in our modern world all these things are magnified—mostly because we are more aware of events that are depressing. The media show us a worldwide smorgasbord of everything from extreme poverty to great riches so we can be aware of our social status every minute of every day. We see the manmade violence of racial, ethnic, religious, and national clashes and feel powerless as individuals.

There are the natural disasters like asteroids and comets, super volcanoes, tsunamis, earthquakes, fires, and global climate change. We hear conflicting messages about the depletion of resources, economic globalism that moves jobs around, the sorry state of our educational system, ethics, politics, the loss of parenting time, and breakdown of the family, and a barrage of hyper-sexuality.

Generally these things are presented to us by the media either simplistically or with statistics that most of us cannot understand because our education has not given us the tools to decipher their meaning and make comparisons. Instead, we depend on emotion, rather than on clear thinking skills.

"Our culture has removed us so far from our evolved style that we no longer recognize ourselves." – Paul Gilbert in *Depression: The Evolution of Powerlessness*

Years of tolerance of rudeness, meanness, and bad behavior have ratcheted upward. Rude children turn into rude adolescents who turn into mean adults, criminals, and terrorists with hair triggers who spew anger into the world. When this seething brain vomit splatters onto others, many react with surprised bewilderment, most with more anger. Occasionally, some level headed person with good people skills will respond firmly and without anger to defuse the situation. A few people will recognize the anger, perhaps, as their own being returned to them. What goes around comes around.

Loss can trigger depression. It doesn't matter what is lost. It may be the loss of a spouse or other family member or a friend, through death, divorce, or separation. It could be loss of a loved pet or of a sense of personal power. It might be the loss of a job, a business, one's own abilities or, even, of meaningful personal possessions. It might be the questioning and possible collapse of an inadequate religious or philosophical belief system. After these sorts of experiences, it is natural and healthy to go through a grieving process, but sometimes we get stuck in the process and become clinically depressed.

SPIRITUAL CAUSES OF DEPRESSION

It is not as easy as it used to be to understand our place in the universe and our purpose in life—especially if we are reluctant to accept whole hog the pronouncements of religious demagogues who are usually more interested in power than in real spirituality. I am not condemning religion that is affirming and life enhancing. I abhor the ones that shout their degradation of spirit as they presume to know what God thinks. They remind me of the line in an old song, "…and God's on our side…" always sung with smugness and finality in the tiny church my family attended in the rural South. Too often the spiritual becomes institutionalized as religion which then becomes about political and economic power. Jesus was about love and helpfulness and forgiveness.

Martin Luther King said, "Our scientific power has outrun our spiritual power. We have guided missiles and misguided men."

Buddhism teaches that negative thoughts and emotions can be controlled. Through practice of certain techniques, we can learn to transform or eliminate them. Indeed, recognizing and transforming corrosive emotions and thoughts is really the heart of any truly spiritual practice.

As we heal from our depression, we must develop—or, perhaps redevelop—meaning and purpose for our lives. Meaning usually comes from three sources: relationships, causes we firmly believe in, and our work. This is sometimes the hardest part of healing, but it is the root of true happiness.

"Part of my meaning and purpose in life is writing this book" D.A. Journal entry

PHYSICAL CAUSES OF DEPRESSION

We have come a long way since the ancient Egyptians practiced brain surgery in an effort to cure mental illness and Hippocrates attributed depression (or a "melancholic temperament") to an excess of black bile in the body. During the intervening few thousand years, well, mostly during the last ten years, we have learned a lot about the brain and how it works.

We are learning how thoughts are associated with physical changes in the brain. Using modern neuroimaging techniques[16] we can actually see mental activity in living human brains, and it is apparent that the structure of the brains of depressed people is different than in those of non-depressed people.

As scientists learn about neurons, neurotransmitters, synapses, receptor sensitivity, limbic systems and feedback loops, neuropeptide chains, hormones, amines, circadian systems, genetic factors, and a lot of other big-word things that are beyond the scope of this book, it becomes apparent that the chemical balances within our brains are extremely important and extremely complicated, much more complicated than ever before imagined—like soup.

A good bowl of soup can be a work of art. It is also a study in truly intricate and delicate chemical balance. A whiff too much or too little of any one of many ingredients can spoil the interrelationships of the whole resulting in yukky soup. How badly your brain chemistry is out of balance may determine whether your mind is really bitter or maybe just kind of flat.

There are many things that can affect the balance of our neurochemicals and therefore our moods:

- Undiagnosed illnesses such as diabetes, thyroid disease, Alzheimer's, multiple sclerosis, epilepsy, viral encephalitis, mononucleosis, infectious hepatitis, some cancers, heart disease, and nutritional disorders.

- Medications, both prescription and non-prescription. Some of the more commonly used medications which can sometimes cause mood disorders are antihypertensives, antiarrhythmias, cortisone and similar steroids, glaucoma medication, and antihistamines. Only some of the drugs within each of these groups can have this side effect, and it is something that must be monitored by your doctor. **Do not quit taking any medication without first checking with your doctor.**

- Alcohol and other substances, both legal and illegal.

- Environmental toxins.

- Allergies, sleep problems, lack of physical exercise, stress, the amount of daylight, infectious agents (bacteria and viruses)

- Learning plays a role in the physical organization and the chemical makeup of the brain.[17]

- A genetic predisposition may increase our vulnerability to these chemical imbalances.

I am neither a scientist nor a health care professional, so I am not qualified to give a professional opinion as to matters of physical versus psychological causes of depression. But I have lived in this body with depressive illness for many years, so I know about depression in a way that many health professionals cannot. I have learned much.

In my opinion, depression is a physical brain condition which has physical, emotional, cognitive, social, and spiritual causes, symptoms, and treatment. It is caused by an interplay of all these factors. It is a holistic condition. We have to get the balance right so our souls can find their true expression.

In a depressed person the physical and the psycho/social/spiritual aspects are so hooked together that it is difficult to tell where one leaves off and the other begins. This is why I use the imagery of the Monkey Wrench pattern. In practical reality, the two aspects are hooked together in an equal, painful, monotonous, slow spin.

We still have a lot to learn to understand how all of these things interact. How do the physical characteristics allow thought habits which would not be a problem otherwise, to get out of control and become huge, debilitating problems? How do our social roles and our learning have a physical effect on the brain? How do our thinking patterns affect our social interactions and the physical patterns of the brain? Where are the dividing lines between depression as a mental illness, a physical illness, a social illness, or a spiritual illness?

Research into the nature and causes of mental illness is crucial. It is that research which will enable us someday to find a cure. Right now we have various effective treatments, but not a cure for these illnesses. Someday the doctors and researchers will succeed in teasing apart the intricacies of the brain and its functioning. They will eventually be able to identify specific discrete things that are wrong with a brain and tailor pinpoint treatments with few side effects. That day is not yet.

It is that research which is also contributing every day to the certain knowledge that mental illness should not be stigmatized as caused by evil, lack of will power, or bad character. We must continue to learn all that we can. Stigma is still the greatest deterrent to research and treatment.

But someone in the depths of a depression or the heights of a manic attack cannot appreciate all that knowledge, cannot assimilate it, and probably doesn't want to be bothered with it. It is like the heart attack victim who does not need a lesson in cardiac care; s/he needs medical help. Now. So, if you are depressed and need help NOW, skip ahead to Chapter 6: How to Find Help (on page 61).

"All this crap about medical knowledge and hope and stuff like that means absolutely nothing to me when I'm trapped in the bottom of that Black Hole."   D.A. Journal Entry.

To read about the causes of depression and then to untangle the causes of my depression from my life are two entirely different things. But it is necessary. Here are some of the ingredients of my mind/brain "soup."

She was just suddenly there, huge and screaming at us how evil we were. I thought her anger was forever, but then her screaming subsided and her silence began and I knew I was abandoned and dirty and doomed, BAD. So scared.

I was always a year younger than my peers in school. I could keep up intellectually but not socially. Our family moved often, and wherever I went I felt left out, unknown, alone.

As a teenager I began to confront the existential issues of the meaning of life, death, God, and self. The framework of readymade answers that I had absorbed from family, church, and culture, collapsed under my questioning. I was hopeless.

In my house when I was a child, anger was not allowed. It is not that we were not allowed to express anger; we were not allowed even to feel it—an impossible situation. Anger is natural. Children must learn how to handle it in a non-destructive way. But in order to do that they must be allowed to feel. I was not the only one affected. My sister has written, "Diana and I both were required to hide our anger. It would be difficult if not impossible to quantify the long term negative results of such an environment. I can remember the explosive quality of Diana's anger as she got older and moved out of the core family. But I cannot remember ever having shouted in anger myself until I was well into my 40s. I simply didn't do it."

In high school I had a boyfriend whom I loved. I was told repeatedly that it was "just puppy love." So I believed that something good and true and real (even though immature) that I felt was actually just a fake. The real lesson that I learned was to dismiss my own feelings as inconsequential and not valid. Our feelings (emotions) are meant to be a very important internal barometer indicating to us whether we are doing okay or not. I learned to ignore my barometer. It is no wonder that years later I wrote in my journal, "I don't know how to know what I want."

There were these things and more, most of them apparent only in retrospect. None of it alone seems to be of enough importance to cause the kind of hell I lived in for much of my life—and certainly none of it equals the truly horrendous experiences of many people who suffer depression. But mix these all together, add a few more crucial ingredients.

At the time I was born in 1943 paregoric was used to get newborns on a schedule of sleeping and waking at the same time as the rest of the family. It was also used on the gums of teething infants. My mother has told me that my pediatrician recommended such use and that she followed his instructions. Paregoric is an alcoholic extract of opium. It is a central nervous system depressant, and one of the side effects is depression. Could these small doses have damaged my developing brain, setting the stage for a life-long need for antidepressant medication?

My genes? I don't know. My family tree has its share of goofiness and horse thieves, but probably no more than usual. A few years ago I found some photographs my father made of himself when he was a young man. I had a feeling of instant recognition when I saw them—as if they were my own forgotten work.

Did my visual sense, my creativity come from him? Since there is some sort of link between creativity and depression, does that mean I also inherited from him the genetic predisposition that made me more vulnerable? I don't know. Did he ever experience a depression? I don't know. I know my mother did, and from what little I know of her family, they seem to be pretty volatile. So did I inherit the genes from her? I don't know. It doesn't matter to me anymore. After all, it isn't something they intentionally wished on me. Where this predisposition came from is almost irrelevant as long as I know it is there to be dealt with.

The fact that I never had discovered that I am an artist was a significant factor that contributed to my depression. My art, my visual way of thinking, is a very important tool that I need to help me organize information. Without that tool I spent a lot of time floundering, ruminating, trying to figure things out, to piece things together. My life is a patchwork quilt, and this book is a quilt too. It took me long to know that I am an artist.

Daddy - 22 Years Old

Nobody Ever Knew I Am An Artist

Here is a map of part of my life.
Kindergarten in California
Learning to work the materials.
Making long wiggly worms of clay
Arranging and shaping them in my own way
The way I know it should be.
Monkeys and giraffes
slowly appearing from the end of the painter's brush.
His back is to me and I keep very quiet as long as I can,
watching the animals and their spaces grow,
learning that two dimensions can become three.
When I finally make a sore little noise from where my tonsils were a few hours ago, the artist
turns and smiles at me.
"Well, you finally woke up," he says.
Oh, yes, I did.

But nobody, not even me, knows it.
My Michelangelo calls the nurse
She brings me ice cream that I cannot eat.
I can only lie on my pillows and watch the monkeys and giraffes
and their spaces play from the end of that brush
as the artist shapes them
the way he knows they should be.
The boundaries of me are open, forming.
Nobody ever knew.....'???

A child in the South, I am 10. Lonely, so lonely.
But there are materials to learn to handle. Weeds, trees, bushes, grasses, vines—those glorious vines of wondrous, exhuberant growth and infinite uses in my mind and hand.
And the undulating red earth.
Natural forms and colors and textures for me to see, to manipulate, to shape to the way I know they should be.
The boundaries of me are open, learning, varied and very interested.
Still, nobody ever knew I am.....???

Junior high school in cool, wet, green Germany.
Eighth grade like a small country school. A few of us and one excellent teacher,
Miss Joy Uhler.
We are a family. I belong
But I am past the age when I can play with my materials.
I hide my creative sight.
I don't care. I am happy belonging.
The boundaries of me are closing in.
And nobody ever knew I am an.....???

High school in Colorado with winter skies hard like ice and blazing blue and heavy purple
Shining on me so fierce and sharp and demanding answers to all the questions.
Who is God? What is it all for? What am I supposed to do?
What am I supposed to be?
Why?
I am trying so hard to be who I am expected to be
I can't find a pattern labeled "Me."
I'm too old to play.
There is nobody to show me that my play can become my work,
my meaning,
And I can't figure it out.
My head hurts.
The boundaries of me are jail bars.

Let it simmer, and all of these things combined to create my very own unique mental/physical "soup" which is called dysthymia—chronic depression. I was stuck, I made poor decisions because I was depressed and afraid to live. The poor decisions became huge problems which reinforced my depression. Round and round and down and down until the slow spin became a headlong fall.

I married a third time and moved from a city to a rural area. I dropped out of art school. I quit my job in a graphic design studio and became a farm wife. I tried to deal with a "put together family." My dog Cindy died. Wheat harvest time came with big combines and trucks and physical exhaustion. Harvest—that frantic dance in slow motion during which I expected at any moment to be viciously struck dead (at best) or hideously maimed (at worst) by some huge and screaming machine whose psyche I could not understand. This combination of events touched off an insistent echo of my childhood experiences of loss, helplessness, and fear.

I made a quilt for my sister Fran. As I quilted, I ruminated. The muted pastel hues of green and lavender and blue which were soft and soothing to her were colors of death to me. They got in through my eyes, went straight to my brain, and sucked what was left of me right down into that Black Hole of major depression.

PATCHWORK
by Fran Stewart

"These aren't quilts," the lady said to me. "These are experiences."
You're only partly right.
If only you knew,
If only you could feel the pain that built
This quilt.
Cool mint, light lavender, pale blue,
The colors of glee to me
Were death to her.
Colors that let me soar, Daedalus-like,
Plunged her, my Icarus-sister, into an abyss
A black hole
A place of despair
A pattern of darkness
Of chaos
Of whirling, churning fear
With no friend near.

These aren't quilts?
You're wrong.
The patchwork of her life is here
The pattern
The color
The texture
The fear
The pain
The guilt.
Her quilt.

Chapter 6:
Finding Help

"Growing up with Diana was a trying experience. To see her now, to hear her laughter, to feel her warmth is to wonder at the box of pain that must have kept her locked inside for all our childhood. As a child, I assumed that her anger, her snubbing of me, her lack of true involvement in family affairs was simply the result of her being four years older than I, and I did not question it.

"As adults, we lived on opposite sides of the country, and except for occasional visits, saw nothing of each other. Our phone calls were brief, for we had so little to say to one another. Our childhood memories of shared activities seemed to be from two different worlds. I recalled people's names and specific places. She remembered swirls of colors and stark emotions and faces.

"Then she volunteered to make a quilt for my birthday. 'Send me pieces of your favorite fabrics,' she suggested, 'and give me an idea of the type of design you would like.' I responded with a request for an asymmetrical, geometric design, and sent her my loved materials, all light blues and greens and lavenders. I did not know at the time that I was consigning her to an intense period of depression, one of the worst she had ever had.

"The quilt is wondrous; it is a prized possession, indeed. But its true value lies in the fact that it was the catalyst for my sister's discovery that she has a biologic depressive disorder."—Fran, 1992

.

As I said before: I was extremely lucky. I was diagnosed with chronic depression and major depression in 1985.

If I had lived in Egypt about 3000 B.C. it is likely that a doctor would have drilled a hole in my skull to treat my depression. Would he have been trying to let something out or let something in? If I had been a Phoenician, I might have been set adrift on a ship of fools. Later, in Greece, and throughout the Middle Ages, a doctor would have applied leeches to my body in an attempt to get my humors back in balance. I might have been chained to a wall in Bedlam, or locked away in an attic or cellar room, hidden from view by an embarrassed family, like Rochester's wife in *Jane Eyre*.

It is possible that some well meaning soul might have dunked me repeatedly in an icy lake in an effort to chase out an evil spirit. Or they might have spun me about on a stool faster and faster until my ears bled. I might have been lobotomized, or tranquilized, or psychoanalyzed.

But I am fortunate. I live in a time and place where my condition could finally be recognized and treated successfully.

Why, then, did it take so long (half a lifetime) for me to discover what was wrong with me? And why do we read statistics declaring that fewer than twenty five percent of Americans who suffer from depression ever even seek treatment?

First, I believe that more than twenty five percent do seek treatment. They just don't know how to describe their symptoms so that the doctor can see the pattern of depression. They may complain about sleep disturbances or about fatigue but never mention feelings of worthlessness, hopelessness, anger, or despair. Many doctors are still unaware of the patterns of depression, preferring instead to look for and to deal with more easily identified ailments with more strictly physical symptoms.

Few of us still have a caring family physician who has known us long and well and can spot changes in our moods and our daily functioning. Instead, we probably go to many doctors in the course of just a few years as we accommodate changes in our address, our employment, or the preferred provider list of our health insurance company. Also, since much of medicine is now specialized, we may be expected to know more about what is wrong with us so we can choose the proper specialist to consult.

Second, there is the fear of stigma, of being labeled "insane" or "crazy" or even "selfish." But even if we are enlightened about the causes of mental illness and do not stigmatize those who suffer from it as bad or weak or lacking will power, we may still be afraid that friends, bosses, or colleagues do not share our enlightened view.

Another type of stigma seems to be growing. We hear increasingly about the over medicated-society. There is a grain of truth to this idea that we rely too easily and quickly on popping a pill to take care of every little problem including emotional ones. But clinical depression is not a little problem. It is a life threatening condition which must be treated.

Third, the symptoms of depression actually prevent us from getting treatment. The hopelessness prevents us from believing that treatment is possible. The fuzzy, slowed down thinking and the indecisiveness keeps us from figuring out what to do. The feelings of guilt and worthlessness make us feel that we don't deserve help even if it is available. The decreased energy may even keep us from getting out of bed. If we have been plagued by chronic aches and pains that have not responded to treatment, we are probably sick and tired of seeing doctors and don't believe they will ever do us any good anyway.

We must assume responsibility for our physical health and choose life enhancing habits. Our happiness, our mental health, is also a result of conscious choice, but in the case of a depressed person, that first conscious choice must be to get medical help, not to try to will oneself into a happy frame of mind.

People tend to have a lot of trouble with this idea. On the surface it is at odds with our frontier heritage. We are supposed to be tough and self reliant, but the inability to will oneself to recover is part of the illness. Seeking treatment and pursuing wellness is, in fact, an informed act of self reliance and immense willpower.

The depressed person often assumes all the guilt in the world, is certain that she is rotten to the core, and believes that she is selfish and does not deserve relief. But we must do something, and keep on doing something about our illness. Merely understanding it will not cure it or alleviate any of its symptoms any more than understanding diabetes will induce our body to produce insulin or reading garden magazines will produce a beautiful garden for us if we never pick up the shovel or the hoe. We have to take responsibility for our own care. We must also keep reminding ourselves that we are not, in fact, rotten to the core, that we do deserve help, and that we can get help in untangling ourselves from our illness, unhooking ourselves from our disordered chemistry, and climbing out of our Black Hole of Depression.

GETTING THE DIAGNOSIS

The first step in climbing out is, of course, to find out for sure what is causing our depression and for that we need a doctor. We probably will need two doctors—a Med Doc and a Head Doc.

Med Docs. There are many primary care physicians, M.D. or D.O., who are able to recognize and treat many mood disorders effectively. For some people, their primary care physician may be the best or only place to start and may be the only kind of medical help needed. However, be aware that many of these professionals are not trained specifically in mood disorders, and while they may be able to recognize the symptom pattern of depression, they may not be up to date on the nuances of the many psychotropic medicines available. They are often unable to identify someone with bipolar disorder. Being treated only with antidepressants can flip a person with bipolar disorder into a severe manic episode.

Med Doc and Head Doc all-in-one. Psychiatrists are specialized doctors—M.D.—who have completed four years of medical school plus four years of residency training in psychiatry. They are qualified to provide counseling, although many do not do so, and also to prescribe medication. Look for one who specializes in depressive disorders.

Head Docs. Psychologists are trained in psychology, usually with a Master's degree or a Ph.D. They can provide counseling, but they are not medical doctors (even though someone with a Ph.D. is properly addressed as Doctor) and are not qualified to make a differential diagnosis or prescribe medication. They can, though, refer you to a doctor.

When you call to make an appointment there is a hurdle you must be prepared for. The voice on the other end of that phone line may very politely say something like, "What did you need to see the doctor about?" That person is merely trying to find out how long a time period to schedule for you. But at this point you need a scripted reply because otherwise your fears and hopelessness and ruminations will instantly take over and you may not be able to say anything, or you may mumble something about a stomach ache or whatever. Here are the words to use: "I NEED TO BE EVALUATED FOR DEPRESSION."

Accurate diagnosis requires both physical and psychological screening to sort out the symptoms, signs, and history of the illness. There are some things you should take with you when you see your doctor:

A Depression Self Rating Scale and a Bipolar Screening Questionnaire (page 86) are valuable tools to make it easier to communicate to your doctor how you feel emotionally and physically. These things may be so terrifying and difficult to tell in any coherent manner that showing him this neat, tidy piece of paper may be the only way you are able to communicate.

Also take with you a list of ALL drugs and substances—both prescription and non prescription, nutritional supplements, legal and illegal—and the dosage that you take.

Since there is probably a genetic component to the illness, it is important that the doctor know about such things as alcoholism, substance abuse, suicides or attempted suicides, nervous breakdowns, bizarre behavior, or moodiness in your extended family. Make a list of these things and take it with you. This will also help the doctor determine whether you are depressed or have bipolar disorder.

These questionnaires are included in Appendix D (page 86). If you are able to go online there is a wealth of tools to identify possible signs and symptoms of depression and bipolar disorder. Some of these sites are listed in Appendix E (pages 87-89).

Put these items in a notebook or file folder and ask your doctor to make copies of them for your medical file. Keep a copy for yourself. Also include any questions you have. In your notebook record your doctor's answers, your diagnosis, instructions, names and descriptions of medicines prescribed, their intended effects and any side effects.

Back in 1985 in our small town the doctor I went to had time to take care of me. Now things are much more hurried which means that patients must be much more assertive. There is no time for chit chat even if you are capable of it. Try to be as well organized as you can in presenting your symptoms, and even consider taking a family member or close friend with you as an advocate and helper. Sometimes family members or friends may be able to contribute valuable information based on their observations. They may also have insights into family behavior patterns that could help diagnose bipolar disorder if the only symptoms you have are those of depression.

Your doctor should give you a physical exam including appropriate lab tests to rule out any underlying medical problems. Patients often misunderstand these tests. So far, there is no specific lab test for depression; the results of the tests will not tell whether or not you are depressed. They will be used to find out if some other condition might be causing symptoms which are also common to depression. For example, anemia or a thyroid condition might be causing fatigue which is also a symptom of depression. They can also be used to rule out diseases which can themselves cause depression. In either case, it is the underlying medical problem, or problems, which must be treated.

Work with your doctor. If your doctor calls and tells you that your lab tests "came back negative," understand that this means some very important things have been ruled out and you are getting closer to finding out what has made you so miserable. Do not let your negative thinking symptoms fool you into thinking nothing can be done. Keep working with your doctor to find the right diagnosis. It may take time.

It may even take a long time and trips to several different doctors to get the correct diagnosis and an effective treatment regimen. Don't give up. You are on the road to wellness.

It is quite possible that your doctor will find more than one medical problem. This is called comorbidity—all that means is that there are two or more separate conditions, both of which need to be diagnosed and treated. This is part of the need for the differential diagnoses.

"If you are sitting on a tack, it takes a lot of psychotherapy to make it feel better. If you are sitting on two tacks, removal of one does not result in a fifty percent improvement."[18] I think that is a pretty good statement about comorbidity.

Chapter 7:
Treatment

Depression is a holistic condition and should be treated holistically. I am a body. Every part of my body is connected to every other part. My nervous system, my endocrine system, my immune system--all of my systems are interrelated. In addition to that, I am also a mind and a soul—full of emotions, feelings, intuitions, hopes, dreams, fears, knowledge, superstition. I am mind and body and soul connected, interrelating. One bodymindsoul. One entity. There is more. I am one entity interacting with others, part of a social environment. Just as the causes of my depression are physical, emotional, cognitive, spiritual, and social, so must be my treatment.

Our goal is wellness—having a normal range of appropriate feelings, not just feeling happy at all times.

Psychological counseling is needed but it alone will not help us out of our depression. It is important to learn about our own particular "buttons" that get pushed, and to be able to recognize the psychological factors which contributed to our depression. But we can probe our unconscious, explore our childhood, understand our assorted neuroses, and talk about our current problems until we and our therapists are blue in the face. We will not recover from depression if that is all we do.

Remember. "When you are sitting on a tack, it takes a lot of psychotherapy to make it feel better."

We also cannot think of depression only as physically caused. That approach is also too simplistic. But depression, unarguably is a physical problem in our brain. The chemistry of the brain, for whatever reason, has become unbalanced. For many depressions, including my own, the key to unlocking the depression is the physical key. This is the place to start.

The quilt Monkey Wrench shows us what happens when we unhook the psychological and physical components:

MONKEY WRENCH

Black/mind/psychological and White/brain/physical.
Which is cause?
Which is effect?
Stop.
This sickening whirl must be stopped.
At this point it doesn't matter which is cause and which is effect.

We will "unhook" the mind/brain whirl by releasing the physical side.
We will use antidepressant medication.
We will treat the physical side, which will allow the psychological side time to sort, to un-
learn bad thought habits, to replace them with good thought habits.

PHYSICAL TREATMENT

For those with bipolar disorder, lithium or some other mood stabilizer knocks the extreme, uncontrolled highs down within the livable range on the mood scale.

For either depression or bipolar disorder, antidepressants work on the neurochemicals in the brain to pull the extreme, uncontrolled lows back into the midrange. They generally take several weeks to become effective.

Antidepressants don't make you happy. You have to do that by mending your thinking skills and personal interactions with others.

Antidepressants only enable you to do the work that you need to do to learn how to be happy. Antidepressants are not "uppers" or "pep pills." They are not "happy pills." They are not something that you can take now and then when you are feeling low. Their effects are gradual and take several weeks to become apparent as the proper level in the blood is established and maintained. Some of the newer medicines have quicker results.

Most primary care doctors follow the rule of seeking the lowest effective dose for any illness. That seems sensible, but in cases of depression it can mean a partial response but not full control of symptoms. Patient and doctor need to work together to find the right drug or combination of drugs and the right dosage to achieve that wonderful feeling of being well without intolerable side effects. Don't give up.

Because our bodies are so interconnected, so complicated, there are, of course, side effects to all medications and treatments. This is just another aspect of our treatment that we must be aware of and work with our doctor to control. It is amazing to me that people who would readily choose to endure cancer chemotherapy with all its extremely debilitating side effects will often denounce the use of lithium, antidepressants, and other psychoactive drugs, even though these treatments usually have fewer and less severe side effects when taken at the right dosage.

There are other physical medical treatments,including transcranial magnetic stimulation, vagus nerve stimulation, light therapy, and electroconvulsive therapy (ECT), acupuncture, tapping, and many others. These are not the first line treatments but are sometimes used for depressions that do not respond to any of the standard antidepressant medicines.

There is a lot of information—some good, some bad—available about the so-called natural remedies for depression, such as light, exercise, diet, herbal teas, nutritional supplements, homeopathic preparations, relaxation techniques, meditation, and various balancing techniques. These things definitely have a bearing on both the physical and the psychological aspects of depressive illnesses. But they must be approached with some valid scientific knowledge and with common sense.

St. John's wort is one preparation that is touted as helpful for depression and is widely used in Europe. Be careful. It may help with a temporary low mood, but it is not a cure for depression. Also, it can interact with some medications with bad results.

Certainly, a healthy lifestyle is important. But just as some heart ailments respond to lifestyle changes and some require more aggressive medical treatments, so it is with depressive illnesses. Mild depression of short duration may respond to better nutrition and exercise, more time in the sunshine, and less stress. Someone who is severely depressed, possibly suicidal, will probably not be able to successfully alter long term habits of nutrition and exercise right away. The ruminations break through any attempts at meditation. The helplessness and hopelessness preclude change.

Another analogy is useful here. Someone with a cold can treat it by natural means: encourage a fever to kill off the germs, drink lots of liquids, eat chicken soup, use steam, get lots of rest. But a person with pneumonia who relies only on those treatments is in great danger. Common sense in this case indicates that one should get medical help.

Many people believe that anything that is natural is good for us and anything that is unnatural, that is, man-made or artificial, is bad for us. A short list of some things that are obviously natural should bury this fallacy: tobacco, botulism, curare, the HIV virus, toadstools, cobra venom, cholera... Enough?

PSYCHOLOGICAL TREATMENT

If we only take the medicine, we may get enough relief from the depression that we will be tempted not to take care of the psychological side of the illness. This is a mistake. We need to take care of all of the causes.

We must learn to think differently (cognitive restructuring) and to interact with others differently (interpersonal therapy). It takes work and guidance, but once our brain begins to work better because of the medicine, the job of sorting through all the garbage in our minds becomes a lot easier.

To figure out how to think better, it is essential to have a form of therapy where we feel supported. We examine not only our thoughts but our thought processes. We figure out where the thoughts come from, how they get into our heads, whether they are accurate, whether they are good for us, whether we want to keep them intact or alter them in some way to be less toxic. We learn how to stop the automatic sequences that pull us down into the Black Hole. By examining and changing our perceptions and thoughts and ideas, we can change our emotions. We learn to build healthier relationships with ourselves and with others. It is not a straight line process. It takes time to make sense, to feel natural, and, especially, to forgive oneself.

Fear of this process is unavoidable at first. After all, we have spent years learning how to be depressed, perfecting the thinking that slams us into our Black Hole.[19] Now we must take a risk, dare to look with new eyes and migrate to new worlds of experience, thought, and emotion. Leaving behind our old ways of thinking and reacting is fearful because we can't yet imagine what lies ahead. A road map would help. A guide would help even more. The map is a plan. The guide is our therapist who helps us visualize where we want to go, figure out what we have to change in order to get there, and provides encouragement when we are afraid or uncertain—and also when we do well.

SPIRITUAL HELP

"For God did not give us a spirit of fear, but a spirit of power, of love, and of self-discipline." II Timothy 1:7

There is a huge spiritual dimension to our psychological healing. I am not talking about religion here. One's religion may or may not be up to this challenge. Spirituality is about a way of understanding life and a way of overcoming destructive emotions and actions. Whether we believe in a supreme being who has infinite compassion for all or feel more comfortable with a strong belief in the rightness of helping others or find strength and peace in meditation or the arts or nature doesn't seem to matter. That we derive a sense of meaning for our lives does matter.

Creativity is part of our spirituality—our innermost being, our connection with God. Creativity is not just for artists. We all carry creativity. It's just that most of us don't notice the tiny sparks that it makes when something new strikes it. Those who learn to notice the sparks and fan them into flames can warm a hearth, create a better business, invent something new, discover a new idea, or ignite the world.

We rush about too much to find out where we carry our creativity and how we can best express it. We need time to think and feel—to know what it really is that we think and feel and to know the reasons behind our thoughts and feelings. Incredibly, we may also need to learn to know what we like and dislike.

Sometimes we need focused thought. Sometimes we need the subsurface thought that happens as we putter about with mundane things. Eventually those subsurface thoughts burst into awareness as the sparks of ideas, inspirations, plans, answers. We must take/make time to capture the sparks—record them and use them. We have to make time, and perhaps a ritual and a place, to disconnect from the everyday world and connect to our inner world. Separation from this God-given world can make us sick.

Forgiveness is a powerful, powerful thing. It is generally understood to mean condoning a wrong that someone committed. That's not it. Forgiveness is an act, not an emotion. It can be a difficult choice. There is some satisfaction in being angry with someone who has hurt us even if that someone is our self. We can wallow in the anger, spread it around, wear it like a badge of achievement—all of which only hurts us more. Forgiveness is letting go of pain, anger, and fear. Letting go. Letting go. Letting go. It's gone. What a relief!

SOCIAL TREATMENTS

Support groups are not dumping grounds or free therapy sessions. They are about community and people sharing information, wisdom, and encouragement. They can be one of the most important parts of our journey to wellness.

Mental health clinics are chronically backed up with too many clients and not enough funding and personnel. In order to manage the deluge, they have rules and procedures that must be followed. Unless you have insurance or other financial means, it is well worth the frustration of jumping through their hoops before you are able to see a doctor. In the meantime, your support group can be invaluable.

Information about others' experiences with certain doctors, clinics, or hospitals can help us avoid incompetent or uncaring ones and find the ones who are willing to listen and work with us to find our best treatment. We find we are not alone in negotiating the intricacies of the medical/insurance/government establishment, and that can be very empowering.

It is a wonderfully freeing experience to be in a group where we don't feel the need to explain ourselves. We are free to participate or simply listen without pressure and soak up the combined wisdom of the group. Above all, support groups are a place to develop friendships and decrease our isolation.

As we heal, some of us want to go further—to become a group facilitator or an advocate in the larger community, or perhaps to someday run for Congress.

   Sometimes we desperately need the assistance of a family member or friend to deal with doctors, hospitals, government agencies, or insurance companies. These helpers take some of the burden off the patient who is not in a frame of mind to think clearly or remember instructions or appointments. The helper's job may be to interpret, encourage, transport, run interference, help gather documents or information, or even help make decisions about the patient's care. They may also need to persuade the patient to get out of bed or take their meds. This list can be long and the work can be frustrating, but the result can be the satisfaction of seeing a person restored to health.

   Remember—our goal is not to always feel happy. Our goal is to have a lot of feelings, a normal range of feelings, appropriate feelings.

Monkey Wrench (continued)

...Oh, yes!
Now see those black thoughts breaking up
sloppy, energetic, boisterous, rollicking, ragged edges, sorting and resorting, finding the ME
in all the many-colored, many-patterned bits, bytes, reprogramming the computer of me,
relearning, losing the red buttons.

See the new healthy Me standing up straight!
Yellow is joy
Flowers are creativity
Blue/green is serenity
Red is courage and common sense
Green is nature and my garden
Purple is God, the Force, Spirit, Un-name-able
The red heart is my center which I have found.

Separating me
from the chaos of depression are three things:
A narrow line of Black and White—Skills and Pills, I need them both.
A rope with a knot to hang onto—Hope
A bow and a flower—Enjoy Life Now!

MY STORY OF TREATMENT

When I was a senior in high school I got headaches. Severe headaches. I was doctored and X-rayed and blood tested, and still had headaches. Finally, the doctor asked me why I had headaches. After considerable prodding, I blurted out that I hated all the things I was doing – things that my parents were so proud of. I sang in the adult church choir, directed the children's church choir, taught Sunday school, took voice lessons and piano lessons. I just liked to sing. I didn't like piano lessons and choirs and Sunday school. He insisted that I be allowed to quit doing some of that stuff. I did, and the headaches got better, but I felt guilty.

At that time my organizational pattern of depression was pretty well formed. This incident of treatment rescued me temporarily from the helpless/powerless pattern but did not teach me the skills needed to prevent me from sinking into depression.

During my sophomore year in college I had to declare a major. But I was confused about what I should do. I just could not make up my mind. I went to a school psychologist for some counseling. I found out later that what he did to me is called non-directive guidance. For the person that I was then, it was devastating.

Psych: "What did you want to talk about?"
Me: "Well, I'm really confused. I can't figure out what to major in. I don't know what I want to do."
Psych: Looks thoughtful... clears throat..... silence... waiting for me to speak.
Me: "I'm a music major now, but...."
Psych: "Mmmm..." silence.
Me: "But, well, it just, umm. I don't know what I want to do."
Psych: "Mmmm..." silence.

This "discussion" went on and on. Finally, terrified, I gave up.

Me: "Well, I guess elementary education would be best. I'll do that. Thanks for talking to me."

Escape! Too afraid to scream at this supposedly wise man, to beg him to help me, to understand me, to make me understand me.

This treatment only reinforced my feelings of helplessness. "What in the hell is the matter with me?" I couldn't communicate. I couldn't get help. I couldn't trust my own feelings or thoughts because I didn't even know what they were.

I consulted my minister trying to convey the grayness in my soul. He was embarrassed. He loaned me a couple of books to read and urged me to turn my life over to Jesus. I hope he reads this book.

After my attempt to jump off the roof of the hospital during my junior year of college, I was sent by the student health service to a very Freudian psychiatrist. "Well," he would say, "what thoughts and feelings have you had this past week?" He was not helpful. He was not supportive. He was only threatening. Do not attempt this type of cold, non-supportive psycho-analysis while you are depressed. It will only depress you further.

Sometime during my first marriage I consulted a psychologist to try to make sense of the tangled threads of my thoughts. She assured me that I was merely "a garden variety neu-rotic" and that it was nothing I couldn't deal with if I got a little counseling once in a while.

I caught a glimpse of a way for me to see, to know, to understand. I began taking art classes.

Much later my then family doctor recognized that I was depressed. He prescribed an antidepressant. "Here, these will help" he said as he handed me the prescription. And then he began opening his mail. Well, the antidepressant did help. But it was expensive, and I was poor at the time and didn't understand what was wrong with me or how antidepressants worked, so I quit taking it. My depressive brain pattern reasserted itself as soon as I quit taking the medi-cine.

Sometime later, my next doctor (in whose office I cried for three hours) said to my hus-band Marvin while explaining to him what was wrong with me and how treatable depression is: "She's like your old farm truck. When it breaks down, you fix it; you don't throw it away and go get a new truck." We decided to fix me, not throw me away! The doctor treated my biochemical imbalance and helped me learn about it. Marvin was my cognitive "therapist". He was helping me learn to think straight.

As I learned about the illness and about myself I made the quilts *Shattered Re*d, and *Nobody Ever Knew I Am An Artist*. I was trying to be whole.

An angel came to live with us in the form of a great, shaggy, matted dog named Hector. My first words when I saw him were, "He better not pee in the house." He was a perfect gentle-man and a lot more polite than I. He accompanied me on the dreadful walks my doctor had ordered—two miles a day. I walked head down along the graveled country roads seeing only the stones and weeds along the sides of the road while Hector explored a two-hundred-foot circle around me. I never knew he was guarding me until the day I stopped suddenly and sat down in the road to get a rock out of my shoe. Within seconds he was there beside me sniffing, enquiring. He stayed rooted until I retied my laces and resumed my walk.

After that we were friends. I brushed the burrs and matted hair out of his coat and treated him to a bit of cod liver oil every day. He continued his self-appointed job of keeping an eye on the house and family and me. I didn't realize it at the time, but his calm presence helped me contain the very worst of my despair and anger—preventing me from spewing it into the world.

In December 1988 another doctor increased my dosage of antidepressant to a level that was effective for me. Finally I could live! What a change! I studied my illness, learning as much about it as I could.

I created *The Ragged Edge* art quilt. It was sudden. It was a have to do it right now frantic putting together of a puzzle. All the bits of myself and the disorder that I had struggled with for so long were finally becoming coherent. As I grabbed at the rebar and wire mesh, and fabric, and buttons, and strings, and beads, I grabbed at the ideas in my head. All that stuff came together in a rush. And, somehow, that stuff that I put together as *The Ragged Edge* became understanding in my mind.

The other quilts followed as I healed in brain and mind and spirit.

I found a support group. Thank you, my friends, for your wisdom and courage.

One day shortly after my mother died, my wise friend, Jennifer, brought me a rose plant. "It's a floribunda called *Cherish*. Think about it," she said. I thanked her while wondering why I would cherish this thorny bush in honor of my thorny mother who had hurt me and so much, gouging gullies of pain into my young developing mind/brain. Nevertheless, I planted *Cherish* in the windy soil of eastern Colorado and tended her as best as I could—weeding, watering, feeding, pruning. She bloomed moderately. After a few years I dug her up, put her in a temporary pot, and moved closer to the mountains. She sat in the pot on my new front porch for three weeks and put out a single beautiful rose. I dug a big hole in my new soil, mixed in lots of organic matter, and planted her again, thinking about all the moves my mother had made as a military wife—making a home in each new place. New places, new friends, new schools, new patterns.

I remembered the move from South Carolina to Germany. Daddy had already gone. He was in the advance party that set things up for the whole Air Force wing to move. Mother had to see to our belongings, deciding what to store, what to ship to Germany, and what to carry with us on the ship that we would be on. On the day we had to leave to drive to New York to embark, my sister was in the hospital with tonsilitis. Mother checked her out of the hospital with medicine and doctor's instructions to take her immediately to the doctor on the Army base we were to report to in New York.

Mama drove. I was ten. I read the map. Fran was six. She slept and cried in the back seat.

After a few days in New York, we had to find our way to the dock from which the USS General Maurice Rose would take us and our car to Germany. I could not cope with the map of New York City, and we became lost. If we were late, the ship would leave without us. Mama put her head down on the steering wheel and began to cry. Suddenly she looked up and jumped out of the car. "Stay here," she ordered, then turned and hailed a cab. She gave the driver the pier and berth numbers and told him she wanted him to lead us there. He did. We turned in the car and boarded the ship. Tough. The woman was tough. So am I. *Cherish.*

I remembered a day much later when she was in the nursing home, a year or so before she died. Her mind had been affected by dementia or possibly by small strokes. She, who had so often bitterly wounded me with her words, turning those gullies in my brain into grand canyons, could no longer find her words. It was as if a whirlwind in her mind blew out random words with no order, no sentences. Yet, on this day, she said, "Thank you for all you have done to take care of us."

I hugged her. "Oh, that's okay," I replied, astonished that she could make a sentence and even more astonished at its content. *Cherish.*

I tended my *Cherish* rose and realized that I forgave her long ago.

I thought about the word 'forgive.' What is it, this forgiveness? My daughter, who has forgiven me for her early life of pain, taught me what it is. I went with her one evening as a guest at her class on miracles. There was a long discussion about forgiveness—what it is, what it isn't. Finally, this daughter spoke up. "It means you just let go. Let go. That's all." Yes.

This was the message of Jesus and many other holy men. Nothing more. He was born into a world much like the contemporary world of the middle east where the cultures are rooted in the idea of revenge. An eye for an eye. What if they could let go of the anger and hurt and just live? It isn't only in the Middle East. Think about the Catholics and Protestants in Ireland, the Klan, the Skinheads, the Hutus and Tutsis. Think about the gangs, bullies, addicts. All those millions of brains with grand canyons of pain, hurt, and fear—long-ago hurts that fly out into the world as anger and spread as violence of all kinds. This isn't just economic and political competition for resources. It is another face of depression. A cultural and spiritual face of depression endlessly repeating.

Hurt—fear—anger—action—hurt—fear
Just let go. Cherish.
Hurt—fear—anger—forgive—changed brain chemistry—life—cherish—love—.
Think what our world could be!

Look, see, feel, think, understand. We can figure it all out by using all the resources and abilities that we have: rational, logical processes, common sense, intuitive knowledge, spiritual, cultural, all sorts of knowing. They all matter. But above all we must think clearly.

Here is my integrated treatment, what I think of as my "pills and skills." These are the things to which I must pay attention so that I will not fall into the Black Hole again.

First the physical things. Take my medicine to unhook the physical & psychological swirl that I cannot otherwise control. This is the most important thing I can do for myself and my loved ones. Without this, the skills cannot work for me. I also have to work up a sweat every day—or at least most days—and remember to eat veggies, not cookies. I enjoy an alcoholic drink only now and then.

The lack of daylight[20] affects me from mid-October to about the middle of February. I try to go out in the sunshine every day and take off my dark glasses so the light can get into my eyes, go through my optic nerve, and dazzle its way into my brain. Thankfully I live in the sunny Colorado climate. Note: Do not look directly at the sun.

In 1994 I began to learn T'ai Chi—sometimes called moving meditation. It works my body and focuses my mind.

I must be careful with my thinking. What I think and how I think can pull me down into the Black Hole or lift me out of it. I must not ruminate. I have learned that if I start "rehashing the trash," I must immediately break the thought pattern by doing something else—preferably something very active or with other people.

Music has power. It can soothe, enflame, or drag me down. I will not listen to the kind that drags me down.

I also try to stay away from people who drag me down. This does not mean that I cannot be a good listener and friend. It means that I must not let the helping and listening devolve into a pity party which will feed my depression as well as my friend's.

That's not my job was one of my great realizations. It is not an excuse. It is very positive. It means that I can take some pressure off myself. I don't have to feel responsible for everything. I can make life easier for myself by getting other input, by giving other people a chance to shine, to strut their stuff, to do their thing that they are good at. Then I can spend my time on the things that are important to me, to my life. If I am not struggling to do everything, I can think, I can choose what is right for me to do.

Know that it is okay for me to want what I want. In fact, it isn't just okay; it is essential. I am still learning how to know what I want.

Sometimes I get to feeling so good that I decide I can control the depression without medication. But I have found that if I quit taking my medicine, I slide slowly into depression again in spite of all my hard work of cognitive restructuring.

In October of 1990 I quit taking my medicine. In November I happened to see my pharmacist and began to cry. I cried because of the depression, but also because this time I had a memory of what normal felt like. Oh, the loss! I began taking my medicine again. Christmas was wonderful.

Again, in April of 1992, I tried to see if I could manage without medication. I slid into the hole within just a few days. My sister Fran called me, heard the despair in my voice and said, "You nitwit! Haven't you read your rules?"

Once again, in May of 1994, I tried to do without medication. I had been learning about nutritional approaches to managing and preventing depression and was determined that it would work. It seemed to make sense—good wholesome food, a diet high in the amino acids which are the building blocks of serotonin and norepinephrin, neurotransmitters involved in depression, along with carefully chosen and monitored supplements to assure optimum functioning of my whole body.

I carefully tapered off the medication as I began my new naturally healthy way of being. As the weeks went by I felt wonderful physically. Emotionally I did well for about a month. Then, without realizing it, I began to slide back down into my depressive hole. My husband became more stupid every day. As he became more irritating to me, I began the downward spiral of rumination. The world became grayer. By mid August I was avoiding people. I was silent. I cried easily. I couldn't sleep. I was depressed.

Finally, one morning I talked to my husband telling him, through spasms of crying, how awful my life was. He had heard it before and recognized it immediately. I will never forget what he said. "Well, honey, you just have to take your medicine so you can get your little spaces filled up again." He was referring to the action of serotonin in my brain. Once I went back to taking my medicine, my husband got smart again. I had to make a quilt about it.

SYNAPSES

Read these blocks like a book across the page.
Dark empty spaces between my red neurons.
See them slowly fill with lavender serotonin
as I take my medicine the way I should.
My flowers can bloom again—out of the Black Hole.

I am still learning the details, but the broad outline, the overall picture seems so simple now. What is right is for me to make my art and love my people. There is no need to be depressed. It is so needless. Wheeee! Just look at those quirky ragged edges!

The End—No, The Beginning

APPENDIX A:

LIST OF THE RAGGED EDGE SERIES OF ART QUILTS

Date	Title	Size (W x H)
1985	Fran's Quilt	87 x 92 inches
1985 - 1988	Shattered Red	96 x 84 inches
1988	Nobody Ever Knew I Am an Artist	45 x 54 inches
1989	The Ragged Edge	39 x 61 inches
1989	The Rooster Crows Too Early	58 x 73 inches
1989	Flipped Up	24 x 44 inches
1989	Flipped Out	28 x 64 inches
1990	Zig Zag	37 x 61 inches
1990	Celebrate – not shown	24 x 17 inches
1991	Monkey Wrench	37 x 70 inches
1992	Serenity - not shown	48 x 40 inches
1991- 1993	Ship of Fools	42 x 37 inches
1994	Synapses	45 x 46 inches

APPENDIX B:

HOW TO FIND HELP FOR YOURSELF

EMERGENCY SITUATION
Call a mental health hotline, a suicide prevention center, or 911.

FOR NON EMERGENCY SITUATIONS DO THESE TWO THINGS FIRST
- Fill out the Depression Self Rating Scale in Appendix D (page 86).
- When you go for your appointment, you should take the Depression Self Rating Scale, BipolarQuestionnaire, a list of family medical history and a list of all medicines and other substances that you take with you and ask your doctor to help you with both physical treatment and finding psychological treatment. This is extremely important.

NOW CHOOSE ONE OF THESE METHODS
Method # 1.
- Call your regular doctor. Get an appointment to be evaluated for depression and bipolar disorder.

Note: There are many general practitioners who are able to recognize and treat mood disorders effectively. Your general practitioner is almost certainly the best place to start, but, as with any other illness, if you are not getting significant improvement within a reasonable period of time (and especially if you have suicidal thoughts) you need to consult someone who specializes in the treatment of depression. Either ask your doctor for a referral to a specialist or use Method 2, below, to find one.

Method #2
- Get out the Yellow Pages of your phone book or do an online search.
- Look under the heading Physicians and Surgeons, M.D. and D.O. by Types of Practice
- Now look under the subheading Psychiatry, General.
- These listings may or may not say something like Specializing in Depression or Specializing in Treatment of Biochemical Mental Illness (this wording will probably include mention of other things such as panic disorder, anxiety, or stress).
- Call and make an appointment to be evaluated for depression and bipolar disorder.

Method # 3.
- Find a local mental health clinic with a sliding-fee scale.
- Get an appointment to be evaluated for depression and bipolar disorder.

APPENDIX C:

HOW FAMILY AND FRIENDS CAN HELP

EMERGENCY SITUATIONS

- In a nonviolent crisis get the person to his doctor or therapist. If he doesn't have one, get him to a hospital emergency room. If necessary, call the paramedics for assistance.
- In a dangerous crisis call the police. They are often the best equipped, most available resource, especially when a crime has been committed or when there is a strong possibility that the person may do physical injury to himself or others.
- Once the emergency situation has been brought under control, if the troubled individual is already in treatment, call his therapist. If he is not in treatment, call his regular doctor, a mental health hotline, suicide prevention center, hospital, or mental health clinic.

Source: National Institute of Mental Health brochure, *A Consumer's Guide to Mental Health Services.*

GENERAL GUIDELINES

- Help lead the depressed person to appropriate treatment.
- Maintain as normal a relationship as possible.
- Point out distorted negative thinking without being critical or disapproving.
- Acknowledge that the person is suffering and in pain.
- Offer encouragement and pay compliments.
- Show that you respect and value the depressed person.
- Demonstrate that you know that the person is suffering from an illness, not a personal weakness.

Source: The brochure *Depressive Illness*, published by the National Alliance for the Mentally Ill.

My addition: If you have a depressed person in your household, get rid of your guns.

APPENDIX D:

QUESTIONNAIRES

DEPRESSION SELF RATING SCALE

1.	Do you feel sad, unhappy, blue, or down-in-the-dumps?	YES	NO
2.	Do you take interest and feel pleasure in your normal daily activities?	YES	NO
3.	Do you have a poor appetite OR do you overeat?	YES	NO
4.	Do you have trouble sleeping OR do you sleep too much?	YES	NO
5.	Are you tired much of the time or have low energy?	YES	NO
6.	Is it difficult to concentrate and make decisions?	YES	NO
7.	Do you think of yourself as worthless, incapable, a failure?	YES	NO
8.	Do you feel hopeless?	YES	NO
9.	Do you think about suicide or death?	YES	NO
10.	Do you often have problems dealing with other people even if it seems to be their fault?	YES	NO

BIPOLAR QUESTIONAIRE

The first part of the bipolar questionnaire is the same as the depression questionnaire.

Bipolar Mania Questionnaire

1.	Do you often overestimate your abilities and talents or feel that you are very important?	YES	NO
2.	Do you go for days with no or very little sleep and do not feel tired?	YES	NO
3.	Do you talk loudly or non-stop?	YES	NO
4.	Do your thoughts race and jump from one topic to another?	YES	NO
5.	Is it hard for you to screen out irrelevant details?	YES	NO
6.	Do you feel agitated or restless?	YES	NO
7.	Do you sometimes have sex with strangers, rack up significant debt, abuse drugs, or make rash investment decisions?	YES	NO

APPENDIX E:

RESOURCES, ORGANIZATIONS AND WEB SITES

National Alliance on Mental Illness (NAMI)
3803 North Fairfax Drive
Suite 100
Arlington, VA 22203
(703) 524 7600
(800) 950-NAMI
           www.NAMI.org

Depression and Bipolar Support Alliance (DBSA)
730 N. Franklin Street, Suite 501
Chicago, Illinois 60610-7224
(312) 642 0049
(800) 826-3632
           www.DBSAlliance.org

National Foundation for Depressive Illness, Inc. (NAFDI)
20 Charles Street, PO Box 2257
New York, New York 10014
(212) 924 9171
(800) 248 4344 (recorded message)

Mental Health America (MHA), (Formerly the National Mental Health Association)
2000 N. Beauregard Street, 6th Floor
Alexandria, VA 22311
(703) 684-7722
(800) 969-6642
           www.nmha.org

National Institute of Mental Health (NIMH)
6001 Executive Blvd., Room 81-84, MSC 9663
Bethesda, MD 20892-9663
301-443-4513
           www.nimh.nih.gov

National Mental Health Information Center
           www.mentalhealth.samhsa.org

RESOURCES, ORGANIZATIONS AND WEB SITES (Continued)

Bazelon Center — Information about existing laws
202-467-5730
> www.protectionandadvocacy.com
> www.bazelon.org

At the site click on Issues>Advance Directives for Psychiatric Patients. There are many other topics of interest.

American Association of Suicidology
5221 Wisconsin Avenue, NW
Washington, DC 20015
Phone: (202) 237-2280
Fax: (202) 237-2282
Email: info@suicidology.org

www.bipolarawareness.com - Offers the *Mood Disorders Questionnaire* and the *Mood Diary*, a valuable tool for both bipolar and depression.

Mayo Clinic Mental Health Center
> www.mayoclinic.com click on Mental Health Center

American Psychological Assoc.
> www.helping.apa.org

Psychology Today's newsletter, *Blues Buster*
> www.psychologytoday.com

Dr. Michael D. Yapko
> www.managing-depression-intelligently.com

Dr. Martin Seligman
> www.authentichappiness.sas.upenn.edu

John McManamy
> www.mcmanweb.com

This is one of the most comprehensive sites for depression and bipolar disorder—in-depth articles, links, info about his weekly newsletter.

RESOURCES, ORGANIZATIONS AND WEB SITES (Continued)

www.drugstore.com and www.drugdigest.com
Both sites have info on drug interactions

www.needymed.com
Information about pharmaceutical companies' programs for free or reduced cost meds.

Partnership for Prescription Assistance
(888) 477-2669
            www.pparx.org

Postpartum Support International
            www.postpartum.net

www.PSYweb.com

BOOKS

This list certainly does not pretend to be comprehensive. The titles are simply meant to steer you in the right direction in your readings about depression. Some are textbooks, some are written for the experienced mental health practitioner, and some are geared toward the layperson. They are written from many different orientations. Note: The * indicates my favorites.

Andreasen, Nancy C., M.D., Ph.D. *The Broken Brain: The Biological Revolution in Psychiatry*, Harper & Rowe, 1984.

Beck, Aaron T. *Depression: Causes and Treatment,* 14th Ed., 1994.

Braden, Greg. *Walking Between the Worlds: The Science of Compassion*, Radio Bookstore Press, 1997.

Chopra, Deepak, M.D. *Quantum Healing*, Bantam Books, 1989.

*Copeland, Mary Ellen. *The Depression Workbook: a Guide for Living With Depression and Manic Depression*, New Harbinger Publications, Inc., 1992.

Cronkite, Kathy. *On the Edge of Darkness, Conversations about Conquering Depression*, Doubleday, 1994.

Duke, Patty and Glorida Hochman. *A Brilliant Madness: Living with Manic Depressive Illness*, Bantam Books, 1992.

*Gilbert, Paul. *Depression: The Evolution of Powerlessness,* The Guilford Press, 1992.

*Goodwin, Frederick, M.D. and Kay Redfield Jamison, Ph.D. *Manic Depressive Illness*, Oxford University Press, 1990.

Hirschfeld, Robert M.D. *When the Blues Won't Go Away*, Macmillan Publishing Co., 1991.

Jamison, Kay Redfield, Ph.D. *An Unquiet Mind*, Alfred A. Knopf, 1995.

Jamison, Kay Redfield, Ph D. *Touched With Fire*, The Free Press, 1994.

Lyons, Albert S., M.D., F.A.C.S. and R. Joseph Petrucelli, II, M.D. *Medicine, an Illustrated History*, Abradale Press, Harry N. Abrams, Inc., Publishers, 1987.

BOOKS (Continued)

*McManamy, John. *Living Well with Depression and Bipolar Illness*, Harper Collins, 2006.

Milne, A.A. *Winnie-the-Pooh*, E.P. Dutton & Co., Inc., 1954.

Moyers, Bill. *Healing and the Mind*, Doubleday, 1993.

*O'Connor, Richard, Ph.D. *Undoing Depression: What Therapy Doesn't Teach You and Medication Can't Give You*, 1997.

*Papolos, Demitri F., M.D. & Janice Papolos. *Overcoming Depression.* Harper & Row, 1997.

Prager, Dennis. *Happiness Is a Serious Problem*, Regan Books, 1998.

*Real, Terrence. *I Don't Want to Talk About It: Overcoming the Secret Legacy of Male Depression*, Scribner, 2003.

Rosenthal, Norman E. *Seasons of the Mind, Why You Get the Winter Blues and What You Can Do About It,* Bantam Books, New York: 1989.

Sheffield, Anne. *How You Can Survive When They're Depressed*, Three Rivers Press, 1998.

*Seligman, Martin E.P., Ph.D. *Learned Optimism,* Vintage Books, 1991.

*Seligman, Martin E., Ph.D. *Authentic Happiness: Using the New Positive Psychology to Realize Your Potential for Lasting Fulfillment*, Free Press, 2002.

Sontag, Susan. *Illness as Metaphor*, Farrar, Straus and Giroux, 1977.

The Dalai Lama, translated by Geshe Thupten Jinpa. *Healing Anger: The Power of Patience from a Buddhist Perspective*, Snow Lion Publications, 1997.

Wahl, Otto F., Ph.D. *Media Madness: Public Images of Mental Illness*, 1995.

*Wahlport, Lewis, Ph.D. *Malignant Sadness: the Anatomy of Depression,* The Free Press, 1999.

*Yapko, Michael D. Ph.D. *Breaking the Patterns of Depression*, 1997.

END NOTES

[1] John Bartlett, Emily Morison Beck, Eds., *Bartlett's Quotations*, 14th Ed., Little, Brown and Co., Boston: 1968.

[2] Lisa Thorell, Ph.D., as quoted in "Managing With Electronic Maps" by Gene Bylinski, *Fortune*, April 24, 1989, p. 242.

[3] Gilot, Francoise, and Carlton Lak, *Life With Picasso*, 1964.

[4] www.nimh.nih.gov. The Numbers Count: Mental Disorders in America.

[5] J.E. Cirlot, *A Dictionary of Symbols*, Second Edition, Philosophical Library, New York: 1971, p. 295.

[6] Nancy C. Andreasen, *The Broken Brain*, Harper and Rowe, New York: 1984, pp. 36, 141-142.

[7] I Samuel, 16:23 King James Version of the Bible.

[8] Lyons and Petrucelli, *Medicine: An Illustrated History*. This is also the source for much of the following discussion of the treatment of the mentally ill throughout history.

[9] Information for this "passenger list" was obtained from many sources, chiefly the books by Andreasen, Fieve, Jamison, Papolous and Papolous, which are listed in the Reading List. Also Erica E. Goode, "Beating Depression", *US News & World Report,* March 5, 1990; "Napoleon to Kurt Cobain: Cultural Legends with Bipolar Disorder" *Reintegration Today*, Fall 2004.

[10] Lewis L. Judd, M.D., "NIMH Report: Putting Mental Health on the Nation's Health Agenda," *Hospital and Community Psychiatry,* Feb. 1990 Vol.41, No. 2.

[11] A.A. Milne, *Winnie-the-Pooh*, E.P. Dutton & Co. Inc., New York: 1954.

[12] From Alvin P. Alzinpsanoff, "The Craft of Survival," *US News & World Report,* June 3, 1991, p. 51.

[13] Jamieson, Gerner, Hammen, et al. "Clouds and Silver Linings: Positive Experiences Associated with Primary Affective Disorders," *American Journal of Psychiatry*, 137:2. February 1980. Also see Fieve, *Moodswing*, revised edition for a discussion of positive aspects of hypomania.

END NOTES (Continued)

[14]Andreasen, *Broken Brain*, p. 51.

[15]This is called basic explanatory style. See Martin E.P. Seligman, Ph.D. *Learned Optimism,* Alfred A. Knopf, New York: 1991.

[16]Computerized tomographic (CT) scans MRI scans, and nuclear magnetic resonance (NMR) scans are useful in giving information about brain structure. Regional cerebral blood flow (RCBF) imaging and positron emission tomography (PET) scans give a more dynamic view of the actual functioning of the brain. Whew!

[17]"Learning changes biological structures and neuronal patterning with profound effects on the subsequent organisation of the CNS." Paul Gilbert, *Depression: The Evolution of Power-lessness*, p. 126.

[18]Sidney Baker, M.D., *How to be Treated as an Individual After You Have Been Given a Label*, Audio Cassette, The Huxley Institute for Biosocial Research.

[19]Richard O'Conner, Ph.D., *Undoing Depression*, Little, Brown & Company, New York: 1997.

[20]An excellent book about seasonal affective disorder (SAD) is *Seasons of the Mind: Why You Get the Winter Blues and What You Can Do About It* by Norman E. Rosenthal.

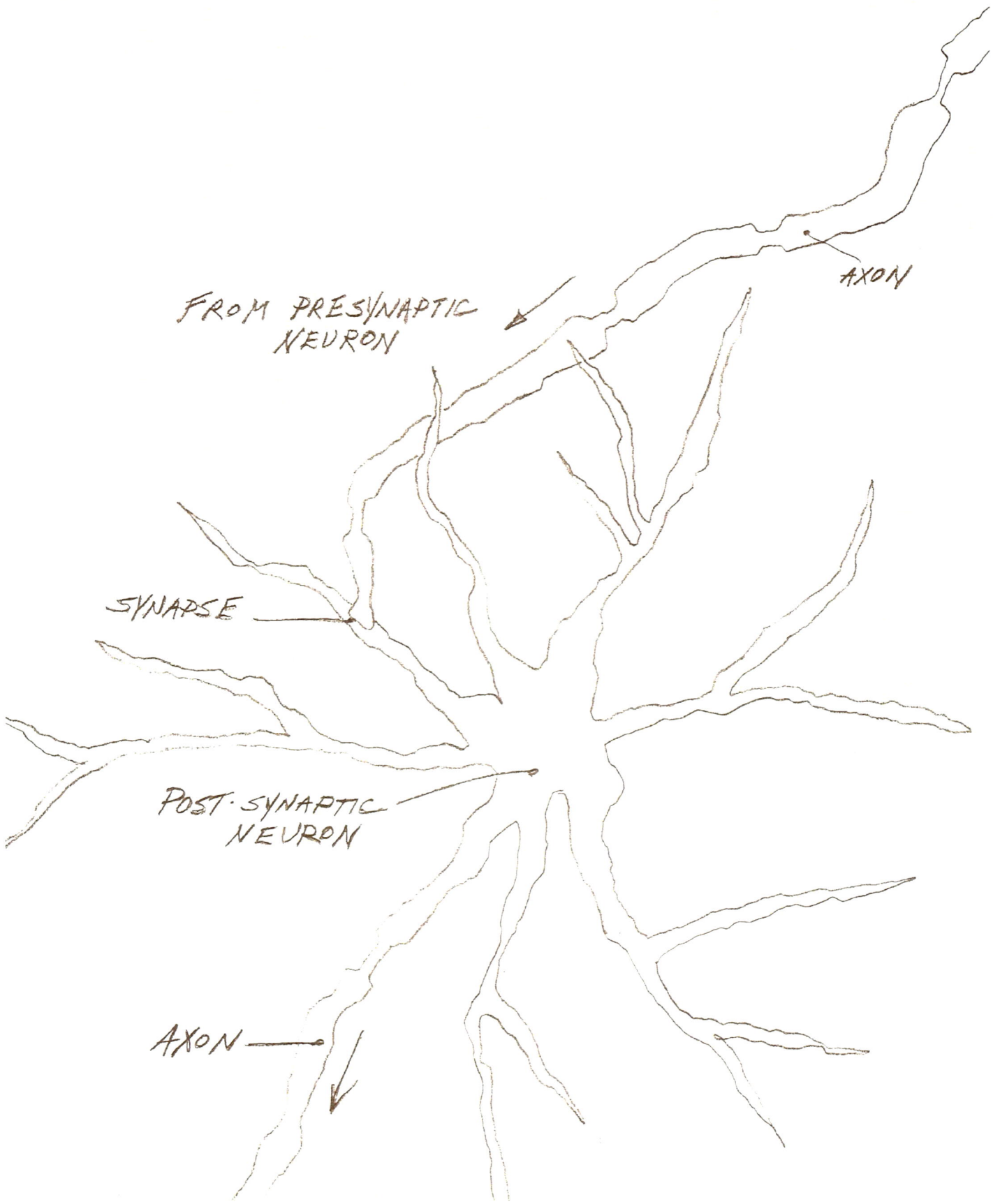

AXON

FROM PRESYNAPTIC
NEURON

SYNAPSE

POST-SYNAPTIC
NEURON

AXON

This extra copy of Appendix D is designed to be removed from the book for your use or to share with a friend or loved one.

QUESTIONNAIRES

DEPRESSION SELF RATING SCALE

1. Do you feel sad, unhappy, blue, or down-in-the-dumps? YES NO
2. Do you take interest and feel pleasure in your normal daily activities? YES NO
3. Do you have a poor appetite OR do you overeat? YES NO
4. Do you have trouble sleeping OR do you sleep too much? YES NO
5. Are you tired much of the time or have low energy? YES NO
6. Is it difficult to concentrate and make decisions? YES NO
7. Do you think of yourself as worthless, incapable, a failure? YES NO
8. Do you feel hopeless? YES NO
9. Do you think about suicide or death? YES NO
10. Do you often have problems dealing with other people even if it seems to be their fault? YES NO

BIPOLAR QUESTIONAIRE

The first part of the bipolar questionnaire is the same as the depression questionnaire.

Bipolar Mania Questionnaire

1. Do you often overestimate your abilities and talents or feel that you are very important? YES NO
2. Do you go for days with no or very little sleep and do not feel tired? YES NO
3. Do you talk loudly or non-stop? YES NO
4. Do your thoughts race and jump from one topic to another? YES NO
5. Is it hard for you to screen out irrelevant details? YES NO
6. Do you feel agitated or restless? YES NO
7. Do you sometimes have sex with strangers, rack up significant debt, abuse drugs, or make rash investment decisions? YES NO